LAY THOUGHTS
OF A DEAN

LAY THOUGHTS
OF A DEAN

BY
WILLIAM RALPH INGE

Essay Index Reprint Series

BOOKS FOR LIBRARIES PRESS

FREEPORT, NEW YORK

First Published 1926
Reprinted 1971

INTERNATIONAL STANDARD BOOK NUMBER:
0-8369-2403-7

LIBRARY OF CONGRESS CATALOG CARD NUMBER:
71-156663

PRINTED IN THE UNITED STATES OF AMERICA

PREFACE

To publish old sermons, or old newspaper articles, is an offence which it is perhaps better not to try to extenuate. Sermons and newspaper articles are not literature. The former are meant to be heard once, and not read at all; the latter are adapted to a mayfly's existence of a few hours. But if the preacher, or the amateur journalist, has strong convictions, and has tried to put them in a form which, he hoped, might reach a large number of people, it is perhaps not unreasonable that he should wish to give his utterances a rather longer life.

I have also been tempted by the opportunity to make myself better known to American readers. If this is presumptuous, I must plead that the extraordinary kindness which I received from Americans in the spring of last year was enough to stimulate vanity even in a naturally modest man.

I need not apologise for including a few articles of a frivolous character. An ecclesiastic in mufti may say: *Quidquid agunt homines, nostri est farrago libelli.*

Preface

The unprofessional journalist is, I am told, looked upon as a blackleg by the brethren of the craft. These gentlemen will now have an opportunity of applying trade union methods to an interloper. I think, however, that the Press should be a pulpit or platform open to all who wish to exercise the "liberty of prophesying." If an outsider is complimented by an invitation to write in a newspaper, I cannot see that to do so is more improper, or derogatory to his official dignity, than to stand on a public platform. If he chooses the latter method of publicity, the things which he did *not* say are sure to be blazoned out next morning. For better or worse, the jury on all important questions is now the whole nation, and our editors quite rightly open their columns to men who think they have something to say to the great public.

W. R. INGE.

CONTENTS

vi   Contents

Contents

Contents

Lay Thoughts of a Dean

I

Literary

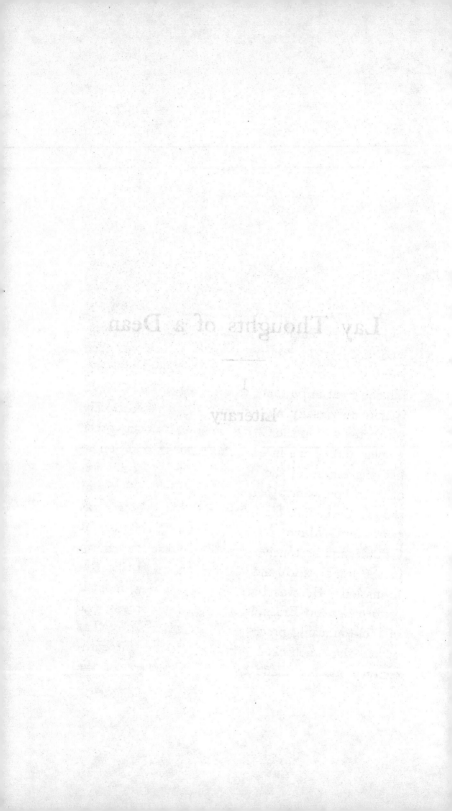

I

JOHN COLET

THE name of John Colet, Dean of St. Paul's, founder of St. Paul's School, and friend of Erasmus, who died just four hundred years ago, is not even mentioned in the histories of Hume and Lingard, but his great importance in the English Renaissance is now universally recognized. He is more closely connected within the City of London than any other scholar and divine in our annals, for in addition to his long tenure of the deanery, and his foundation of the School which then stood under the shadow of the old Cathedral, his father, Sir Henry Colet, was twice Lord Mayor. But his name lives also at Oxford; and he touches closely both the Humanism of the Renaissance and the beginnings of the Reformation. He was born in 1466, a few months after his friend Erasmus, and grew up among one of those amazing processions of cradles and coffins which the unchecked fertility of the fifteenth-century mother made a common feature of the

3

English home. Sir Henry Colet and his wife, Christian Knyvet, a lady of very aristocratic connexions, had twenty-two children, all born within 30 years. In 1498 all were dead except John, the eldest. Christian Colet, who is described by Erasmus as *insigni probitate mulier*, was still alive when John died on September 16, 1519.

John Colet went to Oxford about 1483, perhaps to Magdalen College; but his name is not to be found in any of the extant registers of Waynflete's foundation. The University was at this time emancipating itself from the *claustralis religio* of the monastic orders, and was displaying a new zeal for liberal studies. The boys, for boys they were, lived for the most part in almost incredible hardship, sleeping four in a room littered with straw, and sometimes asking for a ratcatcher (*ratonarius*) to relieve them from nocturnal visitors. But they studied fiercely, for there were no athletics to divert them from their books. The course in Arts was based on the old theory of a *trivium*—grammar, rhetoric, and logic, followed by a *quadrivium*, now subdivided into arithmetic, music, geometry, astronomy, natural and moral philosophy, and metaphysics. The whole period of study for the degree of Master of Arts occupied nearly eight years. It was at Oxford that Colet came into contact with the revival of Hellenism which had begun in Italy, and especially in Florence, after the fall of Constantinople. Marsilio Ficino, the indefatigable translator of Plotinus, had founded the Platonic Academy under the patronage of the Medici, and kept a lamp burning before the bust of Plato in his chamber. English scholars of note, William Tilly, Prior of Canterbury, Linacre, the founder of the College of Physicians, and Grocyn, had already travelled in Italy, and had returned full of the new learning. Grocyn had shared with the children of Lorenzo the teachings of Politian and Chalcondyles, and on his return began to lecture on Greek at Exeter College, Oxford. Colet, who, though still a layman, was already handsomely provided for by Church preferments obtained through family interest, determined to follow their example. It was a natural course to take, for the Italian universities were far in advance of those north of the Alps. Guthrie, in his "Travels through Greece and Italy," "found the tombs of several illustrious Englishmen in the Dominican convent at Bologna, who died while pursuing their studies in that city in the reign of Henry VII." So in 1494, at the age of twenty-eight, Colet went first to France and then to Italy. It would be interesting to know whether he came under the influence of Savonarola at Florence. It is highly probable that he was influenced by him, either directly or indirectly; but it is not certain that he went to Florence at all. His object in visiting Italy was not so much to continue his studies of Plato and Plotinus, as to acquaint himself with the Greek theologians who had made Platonism Christian. He read Origen and Dionysius the Areopagite, and at the same time studied civil and canon law. There was always something self-willed and opinionative in Colet's mind; and he conceived a strong dislike for Augustine and the medieval schoolmen, according to the testimony of Erasmus. His contempt for scholastic theology cannot be denied, but he quotes Augustine so often that the "unfairness" of which Erasmus complains must not be confounded with neglect; and Erasmus adds that he was well acquainted with "Scotus and Thomas and others of that stamp," though he did not like them. He returned to Oxford, perhaps for the Michaelmas Term of 1496, and resided there, leaving his father's house.

It seems to have been a bold, and possibly an irregular, innovation when Colet began to lecture, publicly and gratuitously, on St. Paul's Epistles, though he held no divinity degree. The lectures excited great stir by their novel and almost revolutionary method. The accepted practice in lecturing upon divinity was to torture the text of Scripture, in order to bring out the "moral, the allegorical, and the anagogical" value of each verse. The literal sense, as Colet complains, had become nothing at all. The lecturer would fortify himself by a "golden chain" of quotations from patristic expositions, on the same lines. Colet, on the contrary, lectured as a modern scholar would lecture, on the Epistles of St. Paul as the letters of a living man, drawing from them indications of the writer's character and of the circumstances which called them forth. His citations were not from the Fathers, but from other passages in the Epistles which threw light on the passage which he was discussing. At the end of his exposition of the Romans he says that "he has tried, to the best of his power, with the aid of the Divine Grace, to bring out St. Paul's true meaning." To us this seems the obvious duty of a lecturer; but Colet was a pioneer. In other ways also these lectures pointed to the future. He was especially attracted by that side of Paulinism which has provided Protestant theology with most of its texts, and proved with relish from the apostle's words that "rites and ceremonies neither purify the spirit nor justify the man." His study of Origen doubtless helped him to take what at that time was a very liberal view of the inspira-

tion of the Old Testament.   Moses, he says, accom-
modated his teaching to the dull intelligence of his
readers, and fed them with milk, not with strong
meat.

But Colet soon returned to the studies in Christian Platonism which he had begun at Oxford and
continued in Italy, when he was in the company of
the enthusiastic Italian Platonists. His next book
was that which he probably describes in his will
as "the Abbreviations"—an abstract, with many
original reflections, of the Celestial and Ecclesiastical Hierarchies of Dionysius the Areopagite. So
little has survived of Colet's works that a special
interest attaches to this commentary, which the
author declares to have been written "from memory"—without having the text of Dionysius before
him.   Colet's memory had, in fact, been improved
almost miraculously by a predecessor of the much-
advertised Pelman. In Wirtzung's "General Prac-
tise of Physicke" (1605), we are told that there was
here in England a Canon, a "Doctor of Divinity and
also in Law, named Johannes Coletus, to whom, by
the time he was sixteen years old, was an experiment imparted by a Christian Jew, whereby he
obtained such a marvellous strong memory that
he retained and kept all that he ever read in his
lifetime." But the book, though it shows thor-

ough knowledge of Dionysius, contains much of Colet's own, and its theology is more Christian than that of the disciple of Proclus whose singular fortune it was to pass under the name of St. Paul's Athenian convert, and to become the patron saint of France. And Colet's denunciations of worldly and carnal ecclesiastics, which abound in this treatise, are all his own. But we should have thought more highly of Colet's critical capacity if he had made the discovery, which his friend Grocyn made very quickly when he began to work upon Dionysius, that these books could not possibly have been written in the first century.

In 1498 Erasmus of Rotterdam arrived at Oxford, brought over by Lord Mountjoy from Paris. Erasmus at this time did not know a word of English, but he was received by the Prior of St. Mary's, Richard Charnock, a cultivated man, who soon saw that he was entertaining no common guest. Colet lost no time in offering Erasmus his friendship in a charming letter; and the two men were soon debating theological questions at High Tables. "I cannot tell you," Erasmus wrote to Mountjoy, "how delighted I am with your England. With two such friends as Colet and Charnock, I would not refuse to live even in Scythia." Colet was moving towards Protestantism rather too fast for his friend. He advised his pupils to keep to the Bible and the Apostles' Creed, and shocked Erasmus by his want of respect for the schoolmen. The Dutchman had a vivid recollection of the Scotist College at Paris, "with its filthy chambers and diet of rotten eggs," but it was not till Colet persuaded him to read Aquinas again that he came round to the Englishman's view. That "brief compendium" of theology, in two million words, fairly choked him, and he admitted that his former high opinion of the schoolmen had vanished altogether. His veneration for Colet grew steadily. "When I listen to my friend Colet, it seems to me like listening to Plato himself." His respect for Grocyn and Linacre was hardly less, so that he "no longer had any great wish to go to Italy." But he left Oxford in the winter of 1499–1500 on a visit to Court, where he wrote his well-known encomium on the beauty of English girls and their pleasant manner of showing their friendliness. At the end of January he left England, and the friends were parted.

At the age of thirty-eight Colet became Dean of St. Paul's, an office which he held till his death. He found many abuses, and showed considerable rashness in dealing with them. He was soon "out with his Chapter," and he had never been in with his Bishop, Fitzjames, a bigoted reactionary. Colet

drew up some new statutes, which were a dead letter, since the Chapter refused to accept them. One of
them enacted that the *virgiferi* must all be celibates!
In this matter Colet stood resolutely for the old
order. The other proposals were good in themselves, but not such as could be forced upon reluctant colleagues. The chief innovation which he
succeeded in introducing was that of frequent sermons and lectures in the Cathedral, many of which
he gave himself. He soon drew crowded congregations, and his sermons were a power in London.
They were, however, frequented by Lollards and
others suspected of heresy, and this was likely to
increase the hostility of Bishop Fitzjames.

Of Colet's sermons, three stand out as of real
importance. The first was preached at the assembling of Convocation in 1511–12. Prosecutions
for heresy were very rife at the time; ecclesiastics
were scared by the growth of heterodox opinions;
and Convocation doubtless expected an exhorta-
tion to defend the faith once given to the saints.
They were disappointed. Colet chose the text,
"Be not conformed to this world," and denounced
in unsparing language the worldliness, the covet-
ousness, the ambition, and the gross self-indulgence
of the clergy. It is a tremendous indictment,
strikingly similar to the attacks of Hugh Latimer, a

generation later. A year after, Colet preached another notable sermon, this time before the King and his Court. Henry VIII, fired with the hope of military glory, was preparing to lead an army into France to wipe out the discredit of an unsuccessful expedition in the preceding year. Colet, like Erasmus, was a convinced pacifist, and had lately quoted in a sermon Cicero's dictum that the worst peace is better than the justest war. Fitzjames, who perhaps was not well acquainted with Cicero, ascribed this sentiment to Colet himself, and tried to get him into trouble with the King. Instead of endeavouring to put himself right, Colet now pointed out to the Court how few enter on a war unsullied by hatred or love of gain, and how incompatible a thing it was that a man should have that love without which a man cannot see God, and yet plunge a sword into his brother's heart. "Much more to the same effect he gave utterance to on that occasion; so that the King was in some apprehension lest the soldiers, whom he was on the point of leading abroad, should feel their courage gone through this discourse." It might have been expected that the sixteenth-century equivalent for the Defence of the Realm Act would have hurried off the Dean to the block. But what happened was this. Henry sent for Colet to Greenwich, and gave him luncheon in the Franciscan Convent near Greenwich Palace. Then he went down into the convent garden, dismissing his attendants. As soon as they were alone Henry bade Colet to be covered, and began, "To spare you any groundless alarm, Mr. Dean, we have not sent for you hither to disturb your sacred labours, which have our entire approval, but that we may unburden our conscience of some scruples, and with the help of your counsel may better discharge the duties of our office." In the course of half an hour's conversation the King "wished him to say at some other time, and with clearer explanation, what he had already said with perfect truth— namely, that for Christians no war was a just one. And this was for the sake of the rough soldiers, who might put a different construction on his words from that which the Dean had intended." Finally, the King said to his courtiers, "Let every man have his own doctor, and every one follow his liking; but this is the doctor for me." It must be confessed that this story shows the burly Defender of the Faith in a new light. The third great sermon was in Westminster Abbey, when Wolsey received his cardinal's hat. It was, as might be expected from Wolsey, a very splendid function. Bishops, mitred abbots, and the chief nobles of England rode on horseback in the procession, and,

dismounting at the north door, went to the High
Altar, "where on the south side was ordained a
goodly traverse for my Lord Cardinal." When
the time for the sermon came, "Mr. Doctor Colet,
Dean of St. Paul's," preached about the privileges
and duties of a cardinal. He seems to have spoken
in a friendly spirit about Wolsey's past career, but
he ended by exhorting him to be humble-minded,
remembering that Christ came not to be ministered
unto, but to minister, and "to execute righteousness to rich and poor, and mercy with truth." It
was a brave discourse, like the two earlier sermons.

Colet is, of course, best remembered as the founder
of the great school which in our own day has won a
reputation for classical scholarship hardly less
than that of Shrewsbury under Dr. Kennedy. A
man who wishes to immortalise himself should
found a public school or a college; he is secure of
genuine loyalty for centuries after his death. Colet's
name has, indeed, been rescued from undeserved
oblivion largely through the labours of Mr. J. H.
Lupton, surmaster of St. Paul's School. It was, we
need hardly say, no new thing for a boys' school to
be planted close to a cathedral and connected with
it. There had been a choristers' school, which
admitted other students besides the singing boys,
at St. Paul's long before Colet's time. We can only

guess at the reasons which induced Colet to found a new school instead of enlarging and endowing the old. He was not favourably impressed with the capacity or the good-will of his Chapter, and he probably foresaw that the choir school was likely to decay under the neglect and mismanagement of the residentiaries, as, indeed, actually happened, for the school was almost extinct when it was revived within living memory. Colet preferred to found an entirely new school, and by a stroke of genius placed it under the care of the Mercers' Company, who from that day to this have taken an honourable pride in its success. The school, "for a hundred and fifty-three boys to be taught free," was built at the east end of old St. Paul's, and Colet drew up statutes for it. It was to be a nurse of the new learning. Pure Latin was insisted on; and it was the first school where Greek was taught in England. The Dean was fortunate in persuading his friend Lily, a fine scholar and notable man, to be the first head. The hours of work seem to us very long for small boys, and holidays are forbidden, under penalty of a smart fine payable by the Master. But the Church was merciful, for about 50 days were knocked off for saints' days and other festivals. In humanity Colet was far in advance of his time, for he forbade cock-fighting, which continued at other schools through the eighteenth century. He saw no reason to abolish the picturesque custom of the Boy Bishop, who preached on Innocents' Day and sometimes took occasion to refer to "my Brother of London," or "your worthy Dean." The Boy Bishop received a penny (worth a shilling now) from every master and boy, which must have made him a plutocrat for the rest of his school days.

Colet was not destined to end his days in peace. He had told Convocation that the heresies which they wished to extirpate with fire and faggot "were not so pestilent and pernicious as the evil and wicked life of priests; the which, if we believe St. Bernard, is a kind of heresy, and chief of all, and most perilous." This has not been the view of ecclesiastical assemblies at any time; and before long three charges of heresy were formulated against the Dean himself. He had taught that images were not to be worshipped. He had denied that "Feed my sheep" meant that ecclesiastics were to be given to hospitality. And he had spoken against preaching from manuscript, which the Bishop of London was in the habit of doing. (As regards the second charge, Erasmus hints that though he greatly enjoyed the feast of reason at Colet's table, he would not have minded having a little more to eat.) The accusations do not sound very serious, but Latimer assured his congregation that "Dean Colet should have been burnt, if God had not turned the King's heart to the contrary." Tyndale says that the Bishop of London "would have made Dean Colet of St. Paul's a heretic, for translating the Paternoster into English, had not the Bishop of Canterbury holp the Dean." There was probably a cloud of distrust, in addition to the frivolous charges actually brought; and many persons were burnt about this time on vague suspicion. Protestantism was in the air and the Church was alarmed. Colet, as we know from Erasmus, was not always cautious or conciliatory. When the two friends visited Canterbury, and were invited, as a special favour, to kiss the various mouldering bones and filthy rags which the sacristan produced out of his treasures, Erasmus complied with unction, while Colet openly showed his disgust. Nor would the custodians of Becket's shrine be pleased by his suggestion that since St. Thomas in his lifetime was very good to the poor he would probably take it patiently if some poor man or woman were to appropriate some fraction of the sacred treasure. It was a dangerous time to ventilate such opinions as these.

The storm blew over, but Colet no longer felt secure, and began to think of retiring from his office.

The difficulty was, that he disliked monasteries, and shrank from the idea of living in one. But the Carthusians of Sheen, he thought, might suit him. This was a house founded by Henry V., and richly endowed. The inmates lived under the strict discipline of their Order, with its rule of almost continual silence. But Colet probably never intended to submit to the Carthusian rule. He meant to build himself a little house near the monastery, and attend some of their services. He began to think of this plan about five years before his death, and probably did visit his "nest" before the end, since in his will he bequeaths "my bed at Charterhouse, that I lay upon myself." But he never resigned his deanery; and it may be that he found himself in smoother waters there during the last years. He had the pleasure of welcoming Erasmus's Greek Testament, and More's *Utopia*, which came out about the same time, in 1516. The latter book must have given him the keenest enjoyment, for many of the customs of the Utopians were such as he had been advocating all his life, and it is likely enough that More got them from Colet.

But Colet's life was nearly over. The deadly epidemic, which at the time was called the sweating-sickness, and which does not seem to be identical with any infectious disease now existing, was ravaging England at this time. Colet is said to have been attacked by it three times, and the third attack was fatal. He seems not to have been present either at the great peace service in St. Paul's in 1518, or at the proclamation of the Emperor Charles V. in July, 1519. But he was well enough to visit Grocyn at Oxford in the summer of this year. On August 22 he made his will, and died on September 16, at the age of 53, from the after-effects of the sweating-sickness. Erasmus wrote of him:

"Thus far have I written, grieving for the death of Colet, a death so bitter to me that the loss of no one for the last thirty years has afflicted me more. I know that it is well with him, who has been taken from this wicked and troublesome world, and is enjoying the presence of Christ, whom in his lifetime he so dearly loved. In the public interest I cannot but lament so rare a pattern of Christian piety, so unique a preacher of Christian doctrine. And on my private account I lament a constant friend, a matchless patron."

He was buried at the south side of the choir in his Cathedral, in a tomb which he had prepared in his lifetime. The Mercers' Company afterwards erected a larger monument to his memory, which, of course, perished when the Cathedral was burnt down in 1666. A bust of him in the school escaped the fire, and is still preserved in its new quarters at Hammersmith.

Colet belongs to that class of great men who depend for their place in history on the testimonies of their friends. Like Socrates and Dr. Johnson, he had a strong personal influence on some of the ablest men of his generation, and was regarded by them with reverence and affection. Such reputations are precarious, since personal influence is an impalpable thing, and friends are not always so loyal as Plato, Erasmus, and Boswell. But in Colet's case it has now been made plain that very much in the writings of Erasmus and More was inspired by their friend, and that Seebohm was justified in regarding him as one of the chief precursors of the Reformation. He had too stiff a backbone to take part in any political movements requiring suppleness and compromise, and if he had lived longer might have exhausted the patience of Henry VIII. and shared the fate of More and Fisher. He stands for a combination of Humanism with Christian austerity in morals, for Liberalism in theology combined with reverence for the great philosophical tradition. When the time comes for a new Christian Renaissance, there will be need for such men as Colet to guide and inspire the practical leaders of the movement.   1919.

II

THE LEGACY OF GREECE AND ROME

JUST eighty years ago a farmer named Robey (was he an ancestor of the great George?) summed up his practical philosophy, and incidentally his opinion of the value of classical studies, in the following lines, which I owe to Lord Ernle:

1743.	1843.
Man, to the plough.	Man, Tally-ho.
Wife, to the cow.	Miss, piano.
Girl, to the yarn.	Wife, silk and satin.
Boy, to the barn.	Boy, Greek and Latin.
Your rent is soon netted.	And you'll all be gazetted.

Mr. Robey has found many to agree with him. The classics have been pushed out of one school after another by the desire of parents that their children may be taught "things that will help them in after life." But the game is not up, by any means. The humaner letters, as Oxford calls them, are finding champions in unexpected quarters.

Mr. Coolidge, the least loquacious of American Presidents, has broken his oracular silence to praise Latin and Greek. The venerable Lord Finlay has consented to be President of the Classical Association of Scotland, and has delivered to that body an impressive appeal for the retention of classical education. Lord Crewe has done the same for the Classical Association of England. Mr. Wells is perhaps a dissentient. He has lately shown us that his admiration of the late Mr. Sanderson, in particular, is only the other side of his contempt for public schoolmasters in general. Thirty years ago Samuel Butler's Dr. Skinner was a brilliant caricature of the now half-forgotten old-fashioned classical headmaster, of whom the famous Dr. Kennedy of Shrewsbury was the type. But at present the defenders of Greek and Latin are getting the best of the debate.

The campaign between the Greeks and the Trojans, waged for many years over the heads of the pupils, resulted in a partial Trojan victory, owing to the stupid tactics of the Greeks. Instead of pleading that the ancient civilisation has still much to teach us in philosophy, history, and political science, and that the imaginative literature of the Greeks is still unsurpassed in beauty, they harped on the valuable mental gymnastic and moral discipline involved in learning the Greek irregular verbs, and in writing compositions in the two ancient languages.

They fought the battle on the linguistic field, and lost it. But ancient studies may be successfully defended on the ground that, even when read in translations, the literature is of great value to the modern student. So conducted, the defense is likely to be successful; and we may hope that many will be tempted to learn Greek and Latin after they leave school.

The twin volumes of essays, *The Legacy of Greece* and *The Legacy of Rome*, are not written by pedants crying their own wares. The writers are men who are glad to testify how much their own subjects— philosophy, religion, mathematics, natural science, biology, medicine, history, and political science, owe to the Greeks, and how much administration, commerce, law, architecture, and building owe to the Romans.

Of course, we do not as a rule read the books of pioneers, who by inspiring their successors have helped to put themselves out of date. The modern clerk who reads a newspaper on the way to his office is no doubt far better informed in many ways than the Athenian who listened to the plays of Sophocles or the speeches of Demosthenes. The Greeks were very backward in applied science. It must have been a dreary existence for the aged before Roger Bacon invented spectacles. But it took mathematicians two thousand years to find any defects in Euclid, who wrote in the third or fourth century before Christ. The famous oath of Hippocrates (fifth century B.C.) was still administered to medical students in Scotland forty years ago, and survives to this day in some American universities. Aristarchus anticipated Galileo's discovery of the motions of the earth. It is interesting, too, to know Charles Darwin's opinion of Aristotle. "From quotations I had seen I had a high notion of Aristotle's merits, but I had not the most remote notion what a wonderful man he was. Linnæus and Cuvier have been my two gods, though in very different ways, but they were mere schoolboys to old Aristotle."

Nevertheless, wonderful as these things are, they are not the grounds on which an intelligent defender of the classics would base his main argument. There are some subjects, like philosophy and religion, which can hardly be understood apart from their history, and their history in both cases leads back to Greece, through Rome. Plato and Aristotle are as much alive as any modern philosophers, and it is extraordinary how modern thinkers go back to them for inspiration and enlightenment, as if even twenty-two centuries of thought had not carried philosophy much beyond the place where they left it.

The intelligent study of Christianity is impossible without knowledge of Greek and Roman religion. We generally assume that there is an unbroken continuity between the religion of the Jews and our own, and that there is none between paganism and Christianity. But the opposite is the truth. The Catholic Church was the last creative achievement of classical antiquity; it owes far more to Greece and Rome than to Palestine, for Christ Himself seems to stand above all racial and national divisions. Christian ethics to this day are a blend of Platonic and Stoic teachings about the good life. Catholicism is not only "as old as Christianity," as anti-Protestant disputants are wont to assert; it is very much older, and not necessarily the worse for that.

Civilisation, if we look only to Europe, its chief seat, has grown continuously like a tree since the beginning of history, but with one bad break, the centuries which followed the destruction of the West Roman Empire. It took a long time to make good the losses suffered in that period of barbarism. The legacy of Greece, except for some parts of it which were irretrievably lost, was taken up again at the Renaissance, and has been at work among us ever since, inspiring the love of clear thinking, intellectual liberty, boundless curiosity, and a certain sanity of outlook, which hitherto have not been found except in civilisations which have drunk from Greek sources.

I think there is some danger that another eclipse of culture may come upon us. The continuity of the present with the past is in some danger of being lost. A generation is growing up, not uneducated, but educated in a system which neglects the historical development of European civilisation. The classics are not taught; and the Bible, which has been a great popular educator in England, is no longer much read.

There is also an almost complete absence of social tradition among the masses in our large new towns. They have been uprooted from the wholesome country life, with its healthy, if narrow, traditions, in which their forefathers lived. Neither in work nor in play are they brought much into contact with natural conditions. The result is an all-pervading secularity of outlook and a disposition to look to the State for help which under a simpler social order men are able and willing to provide for themselves. In the following passage a Socialist leader throws down the gauntlet to Christianity and to Plato alike. "According to Christianity, regeneration must come from within. The ethics and religion of modern Socialism, on the contrary, look for regeneration from without, from material conditions." I honestly believe that if translations from some of the best Greek and Latin authors were included in the school curriculum, much might be done to correct this secularity and materialism, which is the result of ignoring the intellectual treasures of the past.

In conclusion, let us return to Mr. Robey's verses. It is not so certain that a classical education is useless for success in life. The French do not think so, and I was interested, some years ago, to see an advertisement by a business firm in South America, for a young man who was to fill an important post. "High *classical* honours preferred," said the partners, who, I suppose, knew their business. A contemporary of mine at Cambridge was taken into a big firm by total strangers, on the double qualification of a Blue and a first class in classics. He is now, I believe, a most prosperous financial magnate.

But my last word must be this. We cannot afford to throw away the wisdom of the past. It is too precious a treasure to be lost.

1923.

III

TRADITION IN POETRY

IT is a long time since I have read a book of
literary essays with greater pleasure than Mr.
Alfred Noyes' *Some Aspects of Modern Poetry*. Mr.
Noyes is a poet himself, and like most poets he
writes excellent prose. He is a fine critic, who can
find something new and true to say even about
Shakespeare and Shelley. For example, it was
worth noticing that Shakespeare, the Warwickshire
lad, felt, as few had felt before him, the glamour
and mystery of the sea, which in Elizabeth's reign
was no longer *oceanus dissociabilis*, the estranging
sea, but the pathway to new worlds and true tales
of wonder. Shelley, too, is exhibited convincingly
as "the poet of *light*," the "sun-treader," as Browning calls him. Mr. Noyes is admirable also for his
courage, whether he is championing Tennyson
against the vulgar and ignorant depreciation of
modern criticasters, or vindicating his own predilections for the poetry of Emerson and of Alice

Meynell. He has made a convert of me to both these writers, whose poetical merits I had not realised before. With all this, he is a hard hitter, giving vent to a strong and healthy indignation. He will stir up a wasp's nest, but he can take care of himself.

He is defending the great tradition of poetic art, against the cliques of literary Bolsheviks, who seem to be inspired by a destructive hatred, not only of their own country, but of civilisation in all its manifestations. The Russians try to suppress what they call the literature of the bourgeoisie, and our young rebels declare that a painter need not know how to draw, and that poetry must "get rid of its music." Accordingly they produce pictures which suggest the handiwork of a very unpleasant child, and "free verse," which can be distinguished from sloppy prose, because it is cut up into uneven lengths. One of them finds something suggestive of medieval tyranny in stops and capital letters, and prints his verses without them; others have different tricks, all equally absurd. They form little coteries, praising each other, and all show a malignant desire to depreciate the great men of former generations, especially those of the latter half of the Nineteenth Century. The word "Victorian" they pronounce with infinite scorn. They chaunt in unison a hymn of hate against all things beautiful, noble, and of good report; and somehow they get themselves accepted as critics by editors who have no sympathy with revolution. We ought to realise with Mr. Noyes, that the same fight is being waged in art and letters as is being waged politically in Russia, a fight not between old fogey-ism and bright young rebellion, but an abnormal struggle between sanity and downright insanity; between the constructive forces which move by law and the destructive forces that consciously or unconsciously aim at destroying real values, at obliterating all the finer shades and tones in language and in thought, and at exalting incompe-tence.

For some three thousand years, poetry has been understood to be the rhythmical creation of beauty. William Watson in a fine stanza claims that poetry should be judged by its own standard.

> Forget not, brother singer, that though prose
> Can never be too truthful nor too wise,
> Song is not truth nor wisdom, but the rose
> Upon truth's lips, the light in wisdom's eyes.

Poetry is essentially *song*, meant to be recited or even sung, as most poets chaunt their own com-positions in a kind of recitative. There is neither old nor new poetry; there is only the good coin and the base.

Further, there is a connection, not easy to explain, between the difficulties imposed by the laws of metre and rhyme and the beauty of the poem. The French have always understood this, and have fettered themselves by rules which to a foreigner seem too rigid, but which they are unwilling to relax. Now the new rebels, whether in writing or painting, make things easy for themselves. A picture which is all out of drawing, and a poem which does not scan, require no laborious apprenticeship. It is not necessary to "make" a cubist or a free-verse writer; he has unfortunately been "born."

The great tradition of the Renaissance was itself only a revival of the Greek tradition, the one tradition for Europeans, though we may admire the very different traditions of India or China. "The poets," says the late W. P. Ker, "are justified to themselves in arguing that poetry has not to be invented anew and is not to be trifled with. Anyone can preach up the ancients, but the poet who belongs to a great tradition of art, transcending local barriers of language, is in a different case. His poetic life is larger than himself, and it is real life."

The strange ebullition of utterly depraved art and literature, which, it must be remembered, is a European, not only a British disease, seems to be caused by the loss of spiritual standards reverenced by all. There are fundamental principles which were once under the keeping of a great religion, which in its highest forms brought all human life into a grand and beautiful harmony. This religion has now been rejected by the majority, who have no philosophy, no discipline, to put in its place. Ever since 1789, there has been an anarchic movement in European society, uprooting men from the soil on which their families had lived for centuries, and leaving them to drift rudderless upon the stormy sea of a chaotic civilisation. In France there has been a Catholic reaction, favoured by some of the chief men of letters in that country, the motive of which seems to be less religious conversion than a conviction that without the constraining and sustaining power of the Church the nation must go to pieces, disintegrated by jarring passions and crazy theories. Even irrational *tabus*, it is felt by many, are a valuable safeguard when the foundations of morality have been undermined.

It would be a bold saying, that all great poets have seen life and Nature under the form of eternity; but if we understand eternity as the unchanging spiritual background of all experience, I think the statement might be defended. "The Divine," says Hegel, "is the centre of all the representations of art; great poetry may be likened to a statue, whose pedestal is upon the dark earth, but her face, emerging from the shadows into a loftier air, is turned towards that divine centre, and reflects the glory of God." This is what Wordsworth meant when he said that "Poetry is the breath and finer spirit of all knowledge, the impassioned expression which is in the countenance of all science." In another place, when he is comparing poetry and religion, he explains the symbolic nature of religious beliefs in two memorable sentences: "The religious man values what he sees, chiefly as an imperfect shadowing forth of what he is incapable of seeing. The concerns of religion refer to indefinite objects, and are too weighty for the mind to support them without resting a great part of the burden on words and symbols, by a process where much is represented in little, and the infinite Being accommodates himself to a finite capacity. In all this may be perceived the affinity between poetry and religion." My own criticism of Mr. Noyes is that he takes certain ephemeral fashions too seriously. He quotes himself the lines of Coventry Patmore:

> When all its work is done, the lie shall rot;
> The truth is great and shall prevail
> When none cares whether it prevail or not.

We have, after all, a number of fine critics, such as Gosse, Saintsbury, Elton, and Squire, and several good writers who are proud to be in the great tradition. Democracy has no doubt handed us over to the tender mercies of the half-educated, and the Socialist *enragé* makes a great noise. But Socialism, though it lives as an ideal, is dying as a programme; it obviously will not work; and democracy is not in a much better case. There are signs of returning sanity, even as regards the estimation of the poor "Victorians"; the wild men are becoming middle-aged. Meanwhile, it will be our wisdom to steep ourselves in the greatest literature, and to see that our children grow up well grounded in the two most priceless parts of an Englishman's intellectual heritage—the Authorised Version of the Bible and Shakespeare.

1924.

IV

ROMANTICISM

MRS. OLWEN WARD CAMPBELL has made a sudden reputation by her brilliant book, *Shelley and the Unromantics*, which combines careful research and shrewd literary criticism, with an almost dangerously incisive style. Few of us had thought that there was so much new to say about Shelley.

What are the distinguishing marks of what is called Romanticism? Some will say, curiosity and the love of beauty. Others, love of the picturesque and the horrible, deftly mingled. Others, a sentimental attraction towards the Middle Ages. Others, a return to Nature. Others, a recovery of the faculty of wonder.

Some of these are the mere trappings which descended to the Victorians, and, in the irreverent words of Mrs. Campbell, provided the fancy dress in which intensely Victorian ideas of morality, passion, and metaphysics masqueraded in the poems of Tennyson, Rossetti, and Browning. Mrs. Campbell, I regret to see, still despises the Victorians, though happily she advises us to go back from them to Wordsworth, Keats, and Shelley, not forward to the new Georgians, in prose or poetry. She thinks that the true Romanticism almost died with its creators, to all of whom something happened prematurely. Shelley was drowned; Keats fretted himself into consumption; Byron sacrificed his life for Greece; Coleridge took to opium, Lamb to alcohol. As for Wordsworth, he simply dried up. Most critics have allowed him twenty years of creativeness; but Professor Garrod is still more severe; in his judgment, all that is of primary importance in Wordsworth's poetry was written before 1810, during the rather stormy period of the poet's youth.

There is a false romanticism as well as a true. The Eighteenth Century, which some love and some hate—Mrs. Campbell has a holy hatred for that period and all its works—took naturally to sentimentalism, which agrees fairly well with a comfortable materialism. Artificial Gothic ruins and grottoes, Strawberry Hill villas, and primitive glades laid out by Capability Brown, gave great satisfaction to an age which had no belief in man and very little faith in God. It was in these circles that a dilettante enthusiasm for the Middle Ages, not inspired by any real knowledge of that very uncomfortable period, sprang up. "Ossian" was the delight of half Europe, and was the favourite reading of Napoleon, who, as Mrs. Campbell unkindly suggests, was himself a mock-heroic character on the grand scale. All Germany was in tears over *The Sorrows of Young Werther*, a book on which few modern readers dare to say all they think, since the author was Goethe.

What, then, are the characteristics of the true Romanticism, which even in its great prophets is sometimes contaminated with the false? Our author tells us that they are hope and love, springing from faith in the greatness of human nature. Christ, she says, was the first and greatest of the Romantics. He first raised love from a mere incident of fleeting human existence to the preoccupation of eternity. He greatly increased the value of human beings as such, by finding greatness not only in achievements, but in the emotions which are common to all mankind. The joys and sorrows of men are what redound most to their honour. Consequently, Christ was the real founder of a new and great kind of poetry, both in art and in life.

This very interesting thought is illustrated by a consideration of the absence of romance in Greek literature. I have myself been struck, when return-

ing to classical books which I had not read for many
years, by the extreme hardness of the Greek view of
life, as shown especially in the great tragedians.
There is an article in one of the Quarterlies this
month on the Greek Fear of Life. The Greeks were
not pessimists, but they were nearer to the dangers
of primitive civilisation than we are. They could
not forget famine, or pestilence, or the danger of
being made prisoner and sold into slavery. They
were afraid of provoking the envy of the gods.
Man must know his place; wisdom consisted largely
in avoiding the falsehood of extremes. To give way
to deep passions was undignified, womanish, and
foolish. "Nothing great," says a chorus in the
Antigone, "enters the life of mortals without a
curse." Violent love was a humiliating disease.
Hope also played a small part in Greek thought.
The thing that has been is the thing that shall be.
History moves in vast cycles, which repeat the same
revolutions. Periods of progress are followed by
periods of decadence, and decadence by progress
again. They themselves, they were inclined to
think, were on the down-grade. Here we certainly
have a typically unromantic view of human life.
The only question is whether it is not truer than
the romantic idea—unless, indeed, we are compelled to identify Christianity with Romanticism.

However that may be, what was best in the Middle Ages was the Romanticism introduced by Catholic Christianity. Their romance was the romance of Christ. Even the heroic folly of the Crusades was Christian knight-errantry, though mixed with much baser metal. Their art, of which the Sienese School of painting is a type, was romantic to the core. The great churches, built when the people lived in squalid huts, testified to much more than the overweening power of the Church. Their legends, which clustered round the beautiful story of the Holy Grail, express the same brooding and visionary devotion in another medium. Sir Thomas Malory's *Morte d'Arthur* is perhaps the supreme classic of Romanticism. Many even of Tennyson's greatest admirers think that he would have been wiser to leave the Arthurian legend where he found it. The story of the guilty love of Lancelot and Guinevere, and of their repentance, too late to save the Table Round, but not too late to save their own souls, is, in Malory's version, one of the most exquisite things in all literature. When we observe the reverence which he pays to a deep emotion, even when wrongly directed, as an error which brings loss and misery, but which can be fully atoned for by deep penitence, we feel that he is not only more romantic than Tennyson, but more profoundly Christian. When the hermit has a vision of Sir Lancelot being borne up to Heaven "by more angels than I ever saw men in one day," we feel that Lancelot the sinner has deserved the honour.

Mrs. Campbell is an insurgent. She dislikes the Eighteenth Century for being comfortable, and the generation which followed the Romantics for being complacent. The fat figure of George IV., and the bourgeois virtues of the literary Victorians, irritate her. But I think we must beware of undue partisanship. Byron, Shelley, and Keats had hard measure from their contemporaries, no doubt; but, after all, it is no joke to be the wife of a Romantic, unless, like Wordsworth, he ceases to be one at an early age. Their private lives, unsympathetically told, are not much more edifying than the Newgate Calendar. Even Mrs. Campbell admits that a review of Shelley's friends is like a march past of the Seven Deadly Sins. It was a distinct gain when the muses took up their abode in happy homes like those of Tennyson and Browning.

If the disparagement of the Victorians were only a way of exalting Shelley, Keats, and Wordsworth, it might be excusable. But it is surely an error to be blind to the quality which Professor Elton emphasises in all our best literature between 1830 and 1880—the quality of *nobleness*. In that generation we see the prevalence of an ethical, exalted, didactic temper, crossed in poetry by a passion for pure beauty. The seriousness of Victorian literature, its consciousness of a prophetic mission, is an English character of which we have no reason to be ashamed. Pure morality and high aims do not spoil poetry.

This quality of nobleness, Professor Elton thinks, began to decline after 1880, and it has not been recovered since. Mrs. Campbell, in her slashing style, blames the novel, "that ramshackle bastard literary form, in which feeble character and diseased action become the centre of interest. The modern play and novel have for the most part about the same relation to literature as a volume by a quack doctor on the symptoms and development of cancer or dropsy." This is much too indiscriminate, but some shoulders deserve the lash, even when they do not borrow the "Idiot" motif from Russia, or the "*Bête humaine*" motif from France and Germany. Hope and love (not lust), and reverence for human nature, the essential parts of romanticism, are greatly needed in post-war England.

No signs of such a spiritual revival are clearly traceable in the chaos and Babel that the war has left behind. "We see not our tokens; there is not one prophet more." Perhaps he is among us somewhere, unknown; he may be a schoolboy or an apprentice. When he comes, I am disposed to think that he will choose to speak to his generation neither from the pulpit, nor from the platform, nor from the printed page, but from the stage. A great dramatist might help us to find our souls.

1924.

V

THE PUBLIC SCHOOLS IN FICTION

In Norway and Sweden the gentlemen's schools have been abolished by Socialist Governments. Henceforth every young Scandinavian is to receive the same education; the consciousness of class differences and class traditions is to be nipped in the bud. Our Socialists would no doubt like to do the same; but in this country a direct attack would cause something like a rebellion. However, thirty more years of profligate public expenditure and vindictive taxation may destroy the upper class schools by ruining those who support them. Already the Public School parent often thinks that he can afford to educate one son only, and restricts his family accordingly. The pages of "Burke" show that half our old families are hanging by a single thread. The Headmasters are lamenting that the families which set the school tradition are disappearing from their lists; the young profiteers who fill their places may or may not preserve the type.

It is therefore worth while to consider what pictures of this most characteristic English institution are being drawn for a posterity which may no longer know it as a living factor in the national life.

Tom Brown is the one school novel of genius. It has immortalised the brief reign of Arnold at Rugby which helped to fix the type of the Public School in the last century. The great Headmaster of the past was a strenuous and enthusiastic person, generally a good scholar and teacher, and a fervent moralist on ecclesiastical lines. He frequently ended his career on the episcopal bench. His fault was that he tried to impress himself too masterfully on his pupils; the Rugby boy was stamped by Arnold; the Shrewsbury boy imbibed from Kennedy an unquestioning faith in exact grammatical scholarship. He was a martinet; corporal punishment, though not so promiscuous as at Eton in the days of Keate, gave the Headmaster a little exercise on most days of the week. Nevertheless, the manners of the Public School were growing steadily milder. The formal stand-up fight survived duelling for about one generation only. The legalised torture which the first Royal Commission found at one great London school declined into occasional chastisement of small boys by their elders; bullying, such as *Tom Brown* describes, became rarer. At

the same time numerous common-sense changes
were introduced into the teaching, and discipline
was thus made gentler.

But the spirit of the public school has remained
substantially unchanged. What Mr. Mackail says
of Eton might be said of her great rivals. "Here
one feels, as perhaps nowhere else, the majestic
continuity of the national life." The tradition is
so potent, yet so impalpable, that it can hardly be
described in a book. Nor is it easy for anyone who
has not passed through the mill himself to understand these little republics, so unlike anything on
the Continent, ruled in accordance with strong
public opinion by boy-officers chosen for brawn
rather than brain, but, on the whole, governed very
well. It is amusing to see how the just and dignified magistrate of eighteen sometimes relapses into
a boyish and irresponsible undergraduate a year
later.

The great output of school novels has been a
feature of the last fifty years. A few, all of them
failures, have been written by headmasters themselves; it is not worth while to name them. Samuel Butler drew a brilliant though unkind portrait of
the old type of headmaster in *The Way of All Flesh*.
Many others have described particular schools, and
have seldom done those schools any good. Harrov-

ians are said not to like *The Hill*, and *The Loom of Youth* was obviously a little less than kind. Of the many books about Eton, Mr. Eric Parker's *Playing Fields* is much the best; it describes the life of the Collegers with great accuracy. Another recent book, dealing with Oppidan life, is spoiled by inexcusable and cruel personalities. Winchester seems to have escaped the notice of the novelist. Mr. Wells, who has a violent prejudice against schoolmasters in general, has made a hero of one very capable headmaster, with whom he came into personal contact. *Stalky and Co.* did not add to the reputation either of its author or of the school which it described. *The Lanchester Tradition* is a clever school novel, mainly about the masters, who are much easier to delineate than the boys.

But even the best school novels do not rise above good descriptions of school habits and customs, cricket and football, impositions and floggings, examinations and escapades. The psychology of the boy somehow eludes analysis. Character can hardly show itself quite normally where there is so little liberty. The liberty of a public school is only that shadow of freedom which, as Lucan says, can be preserved if we choose whatever we are ordered to do. The social pressure is tremendous where there is practically no privacy at any hour of the day. A strong *esprit de corps* forces the majority into a groove, which, as it is a fairly healthy one, satisfies them. A minority suffer cruelly, and are sometimes injured for life by having their self-respect taken from them. It is a time of rapid growth and change, physical, mental, and moral. Schoolboy talk is a queer mixture of athletic shop, free speculation on all subjects, some cheap cynicism which is mainly a concession to "form" and a method of self-protection against unsympathetic intrusion, and very Rabelaisian gossip. Samples of a day at school are easy to describe, but real character-drawing must be unusually difficult, since it is so seldom successful. The grown man cannot put himself back into the melting-pot.

I am convinced that no good purpose can be served by dragging into the limelight the dark shadow of public school life. This has been done more than once lately, and I regret it. Schoolmasters are painfully aware of the great moral evil of schools; it is never far from their thoughts; but they know that it should not be discussed more than necessary. The whole system is designed to minimise the mischief; this is the real reason why the endless talk about games is rather encouraged than blamed. The accepted methods of combating it are to keep the boys' minds occupied with clean subjects, and to remove silently any boy who is a source of moral danger to others. But the experienced housemaster has learned by observation what has now been proved by psychology—that physical attraction is undifferentiated in boyhood, so that proclivities which in later life indicate deep perversion are in a sense natural at seventeen. A recent and much discussed book suggests co-education as a remedy, which is absurd, since boy and girl friendships, if innocent, would not remove the danger. It may be asserted with confidence, to relieve the minds of anxious parents, that the large majority of boys leave the public schools quite unscathed by the evil in question, and that there is probably no society of adolescents in which clean living is so prevalent as in our public schools and universities.

What would the country lose if our Public Schools were abolished? I will attempt to answer the question by a remark made by an American Rhodes scholar after his first year at Oxford. He was asked what had struck him most about English University life. He replied, "What impresses me most is that here are three thousand young men, every one of whom would rather lose a game than play it unfairly." This is the Public School ethics, the code of the English gentleman, which, largely through the noble game of cricket, has percolated

into the national character. I am by no means sure
that it would long survive the disappearance of the
class whose weekday religion it has long been. The
maxim, "Play the game," may seem to the German
childish, to the Frenchman foolishness; but, rightly
applied, it is the foundation of all that is best in
the English character, and it is the real reason why
we have been successful in foreign politics and in
governing backward races. Power has now passed
to a class which has not been trained in these ideas;
and if our administrative posts cease to be staffed
by Public School men, who instinctively "play the
game," or by those who have learned their traditions, I believe that the end of our national greatness will not be far off. For this reason I earnestly
hope that the Conservatism which is ingrained
in our national character will be able to save our
great schools.

1924.

VI

APHORISMS

(I)

THE wisdom of the wise is an uncommon degree of common sense, and the amount of this wisdom, John Stuart Mill thought, is fairly constant in all ages. Schopenhauer agrees, and adds characteristically: "The wise of all times have always said the same, and the fools, that is, the immense majority, have always done the same, the opposite of what the wise have said." But do the wise always follow their own good advice? I have done business with moralists, and dined with physicians, and I doubt it. Besides, it is the old, as Shakespeare has observed, who mainly deal in "wise saws," and a cynical Frenchman has told us the reason. "The aged are fond of giving good advice; it consoles them for no longer being able to give a bad example."

In old times, when books were scarce, and readers few, the traditional wisdom of the race was handed down chiefly by aphorisms, maxims, and epigrams, which stick in the memory. The Seven Wise Men of Greece had each a label of this kind attached to their names. In literary ages, the composition of aphorisms has become a *genre* of literature. Bacon's Essays are merely a coruscation of epigrams, and a large and brilliant collection has been made out of the conversation and books of Goethe. Some lesser men, such as Chesterfield, La Rochefoucauld, La Bruyère, and Vauvenargues, live by their aphorisms.

There is a well-known essay by John Morley on this subject, from which I need not draw, for I have made a large collection of aphorisms myself. Nor have I trespassed on the great collection of ancient maxims by Erasmus. The best epigrams belong to their context; a mere anthology even of the best jokes and stories becomes dreary, and a long list of wise saws is irritating.

The Jews in their later period collected masses of maxims in the books called the Proverbs of Solomon and Ecclesiasticus. They contain much commonsense wisdom for the conduct of life, though our humanitarians must be shocked at their faith in the sovereign efficacy of "stripes." The writer of Ecclesiastes, whoever he was—not a very spiritually minded person, we should guess—had a remarkable gift for aphorisms, some of which have passed into common speech; they are too well known to quote. The same may be said of the aphorisms in the Gospels, such as "Can the blind lead the blind?" "By their fruits ye shall know them." If one of the Apostles had had the gifts of Boswell we should probably have a rich collection of pregnant sayings by our Lord, exhibiting wit and humour as well as gracious wisdom.

The Chinese, I am told, are very fond of quoting proverbs, and many of their sayings are extremely clever. Some of the following come from Professor Giles, some from other sources. "You may be arrested by mistake; you will not be released by mistake." "He who rides on a tiger can never dismount" (a good warning for revolutionists). "No needle is sharp at both ends." "A maker of idols is never an idolater." "Do not take a hatchet to remove a fly from your friend's forehead." "Free sitters grumble most at a play." "When a friend is in your fruit-garden, inattention is the truest politeness." "Everyone pushes a falling fence." "One dog barks at something, the rest bark at him."

Among the Greeks, Heracleitus, the Weeping Philosopher, was a great coiner of aphorisms; unfortunately we have nothing else left of him. Here are some of his best. "The waking have one and the same world, but the sleeping have each a world of his own." "Learning does not instruct the mind" ("No man is the wiser for his learning," as Selden says). "The way up and the way down are the same." "A man's character is his destiny." "We cannot bathe twice in the same stream." "Heard melodies are sweet, but those unheard are sweeter," as Keats translates four words of Greek, altering the sense a little.

A few miscellaneous Greek aphorisms may be added. "Choose the best life; habit will make it agreeable" (Plutarch). "War is attractive to those who have had no experience of it; but those who have tried it dread its approach exceedingly" (Pindar). "The Good can be studied far better in others than in ourselves" (Aristotle). Might he not have added: "And the Bad in ourselves better than in others"?

There are two passages in the Classics which would be excellent mottoes for a book against Socialism. The first is from Plato: "Charming fellows these are, continually making laws and putting things to rights. They always think that they are on the point of finding some remedy for the miscarriages of justice that arise out of contracts, not realising that they are slashing at the heads of a hydra." The other is from Tacitus: "Industry will languish, idleness will be increased, if nobody has anything to hope or to fear from himself. They will all indolently wait for help from outside, slothful themselves and a burden to us." Plato also has a wise maxim against subversive legislation: "The foundations of a city-wall should be allowed to sleep in the earth; it is not wise to disinter them."

Turning to Latin, we find some useful political aphorisms in Cicero, who seems really to have preferred a form of government not unlike the late lamented British Constitution. "A republic is the *res populi*, but the people is not any mob of human beings, gathered together anyhow, but a meeting of the multitude associated by respect for the law and by interest in the common weal." "Nothing is more iniquitous than so-called equality." "Too great liberty, both in peoples and in private individuals, declines into too great subjection." This seems to be true. The best safeguard against tyranny is individual and social self-discipline. "I approve of having something pre-eminent and kingly in a State; something must also be assigned to the authority of the leading citizens; lastly, some things must be left to the judgment and will of the common people." A very fair description of the condition of England between 1832 and 1867, when

Lecky considered that we were better governed than we have ever been before or since. Tacitus, among other terse and biting epigrams, says that the quantity of legislation varies directly with the corruptness of the nation. His remark, "It is part of human nature to hate the man whom we have injured," resembles some of La Rochefoucauld's aphorisms, but stings more deeply. Seneca, "the father of all such as wear shovel hats," as Carlyle unkindly calls him, is full of neat maxims and aphorisms. "He who is everywhere is nowhere," seems to belong to the days of motor-cars and perpetual travelling. "A small loan makes a debtor, a large one an enemy." We should have thought of this before lending eight hundred millions to the French! "A definite course of study does us good, but it is promiscuous reading that gives us pleasure." But we could easily find sayings in a much loftier tone. "It is a long journey by precept, a short one by example." "So live with men, as if God saw you, and so speak with God, as if men heard you." "A great and holy mind mixes with us in society, but remains attached to its own source"—the life of God.

I add two or three miscellaneous aphorisms from Latin writers. "Those who wish to appear learned to fools appear fools to the learned" (Quintilian). "If we allow the women to be our equals, they will at once be our superiors." This is from a most amusing debate on women's rights in Livy. Martial in a neat epigram says the same. "A wife should be inferior to her husband; this is the only way to have an equal marriage."

The habit of stealing aphorisms was not unknown in antiquity. Epictetus in a striking sentence tells us that "everything has two handles, one by which it can be carried, and one by which it cannot." This is like the Chinese proverb quoted above that "no needle is sharp at both ends"; but the saying about the handles comes from Demosthenes. Schopenhauer's famous saying that "a beautiful face is an open letter of recommendation," comes from Syrus, the writer of mimes, the author of an astonishing number of brilliant sayings in single lines. As for the often-quoted epigram about the hero and his *valet de chambre*, Disraeli stole it from Carlyle, Carlyle from Goethe, and Goethe from Hegel. It is usual to add that it is not always the fault of the hero.

1924.

VII

APHORISMS

(II)

THE golden age of the aphorism was the time of wigs, lace ruffles, and embroidered coats. Life was then more leisurely, for the few. The aristocracy followed Lord Chesterfield's advice, and "did everything in minuet time." The art of witty conversation was carefully studied; it had not yet been driven out by sport. Of the French nobility it might be said that their only pursuit was pleasure, but not that their only pleasure was pursuit. France was then decidedly the most civilised European country, and, as in the days of Julius Cæsar, the French studied two things—*rem militarem et argute loqui*. There is a polish about the wit of La Rochefoucauld, Vauvenargues, and La Bruyère which no other nation could rival. Some of their best epigrams are too well known to quote, but a few specimens may be given. "We are never either so happy or so miserable as we suppose." "We are so used to disguising our-

selves from others, that we end by disguising
ourselves from ourselves." "Stupidity sometimes
protects us from being deceived by clever men."
"He who disclaims compliments wants to hear them
again." "When our vices leave us, we flatter
ourselves that we have left them." "The man who
thinks he can get on without the world makes a
great mistake; but he who thinks the world can't
get on without him makes a greater." "We always
love those who admire us, but not always those
whom we admire." "People with whom we must
not be bored nearly always bore us." La Bruyère
says: "The flatterer thinks too meanly both of himself and of others"; and Vauvenargues: "We ought
not to judge others by what they don't know but by
the way in which they know what they do know."

Lord Chesterfield was a Frenchified Englishman,
and his worldly wisdom and wit are of the French
kind. He boasted that nobody had ever *heard* him
laugh, and that he "left it to the poulterer and
butcher to kill his meat." We might not all agree
that "your daughter's dancing is not material, for
no man in his senses desires a dancing wife"; but
we shall smile at his confession that he never gave
advice on religion or marriage, "for I will have no
man's torments, in this world or the next, laid to
my charge." There is a wicked cleverness in

"Labour more to put others in conceit with themselves, than to make them admire you. Those whom you can make like themselves better will, I promise you, like you very well." But how often we forget, what we should always remember, that "the blindness of the understanding is as much to be pitied as the blindness of the eyes!" We should be sorry for the foolish, but "Never talk your best in the company of fools, but talk only the plainest common sense to them, very gravely; for there is no jesting with them." I have quoted, when preaching to schoolboys, "People are in general what they are made from fifteen to five and twenty." It is an undoubted truth that the "less one has to do, the less time one finds to do it in." "Time and business are the only cure for real sorrow." "A wise man will live at least as much within his wit as within his income."

The Germans seem a little heavy after the French. There is a collection of Goethe's aphorisms which are very wise, and of Schopenhauer's, which are very bitter; but both are much better in their context than out of it. From Goethe I will only quote: "The greatest men are linked to their age by some weak point"; and "Some men think about the defects of their friends, and there is nothing to be gained by it. I have always paid attention to the merits of my enemies, and have found it an advantage."

To return to our own country. There have been two Samuel Butlers, the author of *Hudibras* and the author of *Erewhon*, and both have been wits. To the earlier Samuel we owe: "The formal man never smiles without serious and mature consideration." "Men will never utterly give over the other world for this, nor this world for the other." "This age will make a very pretty farce for the next, if it have wit enough to make use of it." In a totally different vein, and rather surprising in this boisterous cynic, is: "Repentant tears are the waters upon which the Spirit of God moves."

The notebooks of the later Samuel Butler are full of good things, but some of them are no more suited for quotation by a cleric than the jokes of Anatole France in the *Island of the Penguins*. "Life is the art of drawing sufficient conclusions from insufficient premises." "A sense of humour keen enough to show a man his own absurdities, as well as those of other people, will keep him from the commission of all sins, or nearly all, save those that are worth committing." "There are two great rules of life, the one general and the other particular. The first is that everyone can in the end get what he wants if he only tries. This is the general rule. The particular rule is that every individual is more or less an exception to the general rule." "You can have schemes for raising the level of the mean, but not for making everyone two inches taller than his neighbour, which is what people really care about." "All progress is based upon a universal innate desire on the part of every organism to live beyond its income." "A hen is merely an egg's way of producing another egg." (Butler was a wayward scientist, but he made some astonishingly good shots.) "Melchizedec was a really happy man. He was an incarnate bachelor and a born orphan."

Philosophers are usually too solemn to smile at their own science. It is all the more refreshing to come upon the following in F. H. Bradley, the great thinker, who died last year. "Metaphysics is the finding of bad reasons for what we believe upon instinct, but to find these reasons is no less an instinct." "The world is the best of all possible worlds, and everything in it is a necessary evil." "Every truth is so true that any truth must be false." "The agnostic calls his Unknowable God, because he does not know what the devil else to call it."

Those who are not fond of episcopal biographies (most of them are certainly very dull!) may miss the delightful collection of wise sayings by Bishop

Creighton collected by his widow. "There is nothing in life except to enjoy what one is doing. It is the only secret of happiness." "European supremacy is moral, not intellectual." "England is the most artificial of States; a single disaster might crush her." "The Universities are a sort of lunatic asylum for keeping young men out of mischief." "Socialism will only be possible when we are all perfect, and then it will not be needed." "An Englishman is not only without ideas; he hates an idea when he sees it." "In dealing with ourselves, after we have let the ape and tiger die, there remains the donkey, a more intractable and enduring animal." "The two chief means of teaching are exaggeration and paradox." "It is wonderful how little mischief we can do with all our trouble." "Vulgarity is an inadequate conception of the art of living." "We cannot improve the world faster than we improve ourselves." There are others equally good. But what cruelty to make this brilliant man a Bishop, whose main duties, according to a former Prime Minister, are to suffer fools gladly, and to answer letters by return of post!

Another clever writer of aphorisms was the late Churton Collins, an able critic who, I believe, did not show much worldly wisdom in the conduct of his affairs. "A fool often fails, because he thinks what is difficult is easy, and a wise man because he thinks what is easy is difficult." "Never trust a man who speaks well of everybody." (A hard saying—but where should we be if there was no one to expose the rascals?) "We make more enemies by what we say than friends by what we do." "Never trouble the waters in which you intend to fish." "If men were as unselfish as women, women would very soon become more selfish than men." "A wise man, like the moon, only shows his bright side to the world."

Nietzsche is responsible for the saying: "There has been only one Christian, and he died upon the Cross," and Lecky (I think) for the wise epigram that the art of politics is to hear, not those who talk, but those who are silent. Of ambition he says very truly, that it may be either the luxury of the happy, or the distraction of the miserable.

1924.

VIII

LETTER WRITING

THE last volume of the new edition of Byron's Letters, and the little collection of letters, with an introduction on the history and art of letter-writing, by Professor Saintsbury, will recall the attention of many readers to a delightful branch of literature, which, to all appearance, has had its day. We have often been told that the penny post killed real letter-writing. But the two-penny post does not seem to have improved the quality or to have seriously diminished the quantity of letters which are certainly not literature.

The typewriter and the telephone are enemies of correspondence which we shall always have with us. I have indeed, a few occasional correspondents, including three theologians, who are, in this respect at least, imitators of Dean Stanley, whose manuscripts were too much even for Mr. Murray's compositors. It is a mercy that these divines have taken to the typewriter; but in most cases a typed letter is a chilly and repellent substitute for the written word.

Byron, I believe, said that his handwriting was as bad as his character, which is hardly possible, since his letters have been deciphered; but, as a rule, I think the writers of good letters have written them legibly.

Worse than the telephone and the postcard is the pose of being overworked. We do not really get through more sound work than our grandfathers; but we make a conscience of being always in a hurry—unless, indeed, we are trade unionists, with whom the charge of hurrying is a deadly reproach. We can travel much faster than our grandfathers, and accordingly, we waste much more time in going from place to place. Time-saving inventions have much to answer for in shortening our leisure.

These changes, to be sure, ought to encourage the short letter, of which several admirable examples are preserved. The dispatch of a Captain Walton: "Spanish fleet taken and destroyed, as per margin," would have been excellent, if it had been true; the Spaniards, I believe, said that it was not. A Royal duke is said to have written to an Irish bishop: "Dear Cork,—Please ordain Stanhope.—Yours, York"; to which the reply was: "Dear York,—Stanhope's ordained.—Yours, Cork."

It is said that Archbishop Temple once received a letter from an officious correspondent, enclosing two utterances of the Archbishop which flatly contradicted each other, and asking for an explanation. The reply was: "Dear Sir,—Both were right."

I have heard (but I don't believe this story) that during the war the Foreign Office was obliged to employ one or two temporary clerks whose training had been commercial rather than diplomatic. A dignified foreign ambassador was astonished to receive the following missive: "Dear Sir,—Yours to hand, and contents noted. Our Lord C—— has the matter in hand."

As a last example of the short letter—a masterpiece—a father told his son at school that he was too busy to read long letters, and requested the boy to be brief. The answer was a model of terseness: "S.O.S., L.S.D., R.S.V.P." The first two of these are old stories, long before the days of postcards.

The long letter is not extinct, but in my experience it is confined to that amazing species of cranks who, without any introduction or excuse, cover whole quires of paper with epistolary essays addressed to men who happen for the time to be in the public eye, expounding at length their views on theology, politics, and what not, and apparently expect their victims to read and answer them.

Really interesting letters, which make breakfast a pleasure, are rare indeed.

Professor Saintsbury does justice to the ancient Romans as the founders of good letter-writing. It is a pity that he has not given us one or two specimens of Cicero. Cicero's are admirable letters, brimful of matter, whereas Mme. de Sévigné is as good at writing cleverly about nothing as a French cook is at making dishes out of nothing. Pliny is another admirable correspondent, and a most estimable gentleman, as he wishes us to observe.

But the eighteenth century was the golden age of letter-writing, both in England and in France. The French are right, perhaps, in thinking that Mme. de Sévigné has never been surpassed; but if we consider matter as well as manner, some of our English writers are more interesting. Pope is amazingly clever, but spiteful and disingenuous beyond description. And what are we to think of a man who could append to a sort of love-letter the request: "When this letter is printed for the wit of it, pray take care that what is underlined be printed in a different character!"

Swift, that savage and unholy genius, as Lord Morley calls him, wrote masses of letters to two unlucky ladies whom he loved in a morbid and unmanly fashion. Brilliant as the *Letters to Stella* are, I cannot agree with Professor Saintsbury that Swift was "one of the greatest lovers in the world." He had no full-blooded love to give.

Cowper, the poet, is one of the very best letter-writers. When not under the cloud of religious melancholy he was the most genial and affectionate of men, and his judgments on public affairs are remarkably shrewd for a man of his habits.

Horace Walpole is not a favourite of mine. He was a selfish and self-indulgent fellow, battening on rich sinecures, who evidently wrote to show how clever he was. There is not much to show that he really cared about his correspondents.

Far more delightful, to my mind, are the letters of Gray, poet, scholar, and recluse, who gave his correspondents the best of a well-stored mind, and is particularly good in describing his travels—not an easy thing to do really well. His letters are like very good talk, which is what letters ought to be.

For this reason some of the best letter-writers have been women. Lady Mary Wortley Montagu, in the eighteenth century, is admirable; and in the nineteenth two women who married geniuses, Mrs. Carlyle and Mrs. Browning, wrote even better letters than their husbands. Mrs. Carlyle was a little spiteful, but this is not an unmixed drawback in a letter.

Shelley, Keats and Byron are all famous let-ter-writers. I prefer Shelley of the three. Byron is revealed in this last volume as a very im-perfect kind of gentleman. He not only kissed and told, but seems to prefer the latter to the former.

Fitzgerald, the translator of Omar Khayyam, is a prince among letter-writers. It is really a good thing that a few able men should be content to be very leisurely. Their work gains in quality, and they have time, if they choose, to write letters which deserve to be classics.

The modern biography is usually swollen to twice its proper size by unnecessary and dull letters. To print love-letters is an outrage; and nobody wants to know the first impressions of Lucerne, dutifully written home by a young traveller. A biographer once confided to me that all the really interesting letters had had to be left out.

It only remains to mention that peculiar branch of letter-writing—letters sent to newspapers. It once fell to my lot to propose the prosperity of a newspaper which had been giving me a bad time in its correspondence columns. I congratulated the editor on his wisdom in allowing the least intelli-gent of his readers to let off steam in this way. Considering the letters which are printed—say, in

the religious weeklies—one wonders what the rejected addresses can be like.

We must hope, without much confidence, that the
graceful and gentle art of letter-writing may have
another flowering time among us.

1922.

IX

DIARIES

THE motives for writing autobiographies are various. Sometimes, as we have seen recently, the writer is tempted by a big cheque. In other cases he or she is conscious of having had an interesting life, and wishes the public to share the interest. Some men—especially Deans, I regret to say—are raconteurs, and so fond of their own stories that they do not like to think that they may perish with them. The relief of the raconteur's family when the fifty-times-told tale is at last fixed in black and white, and presumably done with, must be immense.

Others have a grievance, and wish posterity to know why they were elbowed out of office, who was really responsible for the miscarriage of a military expedition, who was the real author of a literary or scientific discovery, and so on. Classical scholars have admired the dignity of Thucydides in not giving his own story of the reverse at Amphipolis, where he was commander.

Others again have left memoirs which they intended or hoped would be published after their deaths, and in which they have inserted as much venom as they knew how, conscious that they themselves will not be able to be called to account, nor perhaps their victims to vindicate their reputation. I have no doubt that Creevey was one of these malicious diarists; there is evidence that he thought his papers "would be of great value" hereafter. Some of the worst parts of his journal have not been printed, and perhaps never will be. Mark Pattison's Memoirs were clearly intended to take a posthumous revenge upon the college which passed him over, very improperly it must be said, for the headship, and on certain people in the University of Oxford whom he disliked.

Sometimes the autobiography seems to be prompted by sheer vanity. Vanity, unlike pride, is a rather amiable foible; a vain man is seldom unpopular, partly because he shows that he cares for the good opinion of others. But the vain man is essentially an actor. If he is not posing for others, he struts and smirks to gratify himself. As an autobiographer he partially fails by telling too many lies. As Napoleon said of one of his colleagues, "He lies too much. It is well to lie sometimes; *mais toujours, c'est trop.*"

It is impossible, for example, to know when Benvenuto Cellini is telling the truth. Did he really plant that knife so neatly in the nape of his enemy's neck? Did another enemy really try to poison him with a powdered diamond, and did Benvenuto only escape because the hired murderer, not being a conscientious man, pocketed the diamond and gave Cellini powdered glass instead? We shall never know. Cellini is a most amusing fellow, anyhow. It is good fun to have (vicariously, of course) an occasional complete holiday from all the Ten Commandments.

Colley Cibber was a very vain man, who is commonly supposed to be merely ridiculous. I do not see it; his autobiography is a very good book, which on the whole makes me like and respect the writer. Of the most famous of all autobiographies, Rousseau's *Confessions*, it is almost painful to speak. I doubt whether he lies much; his profoundly diseased nature makes him shameless, and he seems really to believe that his odious character was a very favourable specimen of human nature. Another vain autobiographer, whose ponderous book teems with unconscious humour, is the philosopher Herbert Spencer. This is a severely truthful portrait of a typically English character, analysed by himself with scientific accuracy. One puts it down with a great respect for the man, and with a wry smile.

John Stuart Mill wrote another scientific auto-biography, partly with the object of tracing the effect on the character of the peculiar system of education applied to him by his father, that tre-mendous old gentleman James Mill. But we are also amused by his laudations of his wife's wit and wisdom. The good lady clearly showed her wit by echoing her husband's wisdom.

Ruskin, Carlyle, and Renan have also told us much about their own early lives. Gibbon's auto-biography pleases us because it is a perfect example of how a much limited man, by an extremely wise laying out of his life, can produce just that great thing which was in him to do. We laugh at the young gallant, who "sighed as a lover but obeyed as a son"; but the laugh is at last on his side, for whoever made fewer mistakes in the conduct of life, assuming that the object of life is to plan something great and to achieve it?

Religious meditations are another class of auto-biography. One may hesitate whether to give the palm to Marcus Aurelius or to St. Augustine. The supreme merit of the Stoic Emperor's little book is that it was written, as he says, "to himself." It was not intended for any other eyes. This gives it a supreme sincerity which all can recognise; and so important is bare sincerity in the spiritual life that his meditations are still read eagerly by all classes, in all faiths, and in all countries.

Augustine's *Confessions* is a greater book, but it was written for publication, long after the events which it describes. If we check it by the short, seldom read dialogues written at the time of his conversion, we see how treacherous memory is when it plays upon our own past, especially on our own past thoughts.

Reminiscences are not the perfect autobiography. The present modifies the past by interpreting it. We want the text without the commentary. How did his life appear to the great man before he knew that he was great?

A diary ought to be a perfectly honest auto-biography, written from day to day, and therefore as true as an uncensored war correspondence. We have already half forgotten our hopes and fears at various periods during the war, and we have wholly forgotten our state of mind in July, 1914. When we look back at our diaries (if we keep them) during any crisis of our lives, we shall have some surprises. We have come to tell the story differently to ourselves. We pride ourselves on our foresight, though what happened was a mere stroke of luck, and we narrowly escaped some disastrous decision.

And yet, are diaries above suspicion? Some men look forward to having their biographies written, and bequeath to their wives or best friends an edifying journal, in which they pose as much as they do at their dinner tables. Others reflect that they may have no opportunity of destroying their diaries, and are careful not to write in them anything that would distress their families. I am not thinking so much of what are politely called indiscretions, as of harsh judgments which may be highly characteristic of the writer, confidential secrets told by others, and confessions of one's own faults. ("I am sometimes troubled," said Boswell, "by a disposition to stinginess." "So am I," replied Johnson, "but I do not tell it.") Even in the happiest marriage there may be a few reserves, and no man would willingly contemplate that these should be torn aside as his wife reads his diary the week after his death. It follows that even in a diary we cannot be sure of getting a full revelation of a man's character; and most people fill their journals with ephemeral details which have no permanent interest whatever.

If, however, a man writes a diary which he feels sure that nobody will ever see except himself, he is probably perfectly truthful. There is no motive for being otherwise. He is no more ashamed of recording his actions, good and bad, just as they happened, than of seeing himself in his bath. So down it all goes, as in the famous diary of Samuel Pepys, which he wrote in a cypher which he was confident that nobody would take the trouble to read. I know no other diary to be compared with it.

We are sometimes shocked, but more often amused. "Went to church this morning. Excellent sermon, but distracted by back view of pretty girl in the pew in front. Offered her a hymn-book to make her turn round. Front view disappointing, and looked cross. Plate instead of offertory-bag. Nuisance. Had to give half-a-crown. Must remember to put sixpences in my pocket." That is a slightly modernised version of what we find everywhere in Pepys. It is a human—all too human—document, the record of what Matthew Arnold calls an "average sensual man"; though we must remember, to do the volatile Samuel justice, that he lived in the most dissolute age of English history.

Leslie Stephen wanted everyone to leave his autobiography tied up with his will. I am afraid most of us would find the compilation rather embarrassing.

1922.

X

THE ENGLISH LANGUAGE

IT is rumoured that the Americans are about to propose the appointment of a representative joint commission of the English-speaking peoples in order to standardise the English language. Such a scheme ought to be warmly taken up in our country, for several reasons.

It would check the further divergence of speech and writing on the two sides of the Atlantic. Some undesirable innovations in both countries might be ruled out; and in cases where different usages were pronounced to be both admissible, the divergences would be noted in a way which would prevent misunderstandings. Such misunderstandings are not infrequent. It is a small thing that the Americans use "spool" for "reel," "suspenders" for "braces," "elevator" for "lift"; these things are easily learnt by the traveller. But other variations in the meaning of words are occasionally awkward. I give a few examples:

In England		In America
Nasty	Unpleasant.	Disgusting.
Homely	Unsophisticated.	Ugly.
Billion	A million millions.	A thousand millions.
Hypothecate	To pawn.	To frame an hypothesis.
Politician	A would-be statesman.	A political agent.

Several other examples might be found.

Secondly, the commission might arrest the degradation of the language which is in constant progress, now that everybody writes and very few take any thought for style. The French have their famous Academy, to belong to which is the ambition of every man of letters. A man who writes slipshod French, or uses words which have not been accepted into the literary language, has no chance of being elected an Academician. Consequently, the art of composition is taken much more seriously in France than it is with us. We have a British Academy, but it is more concerned with the matter than with the manner of writing.

The commission would, I suppose, consider and report upon the pronunciation of English as well as correctness of diction in writing. Pronunciation in English is very vague, and our unique method of spelling is the despair of foreigners who wish to learn from books how to speak our language. The Poet Laureate has counted no less than twenty-one different spellings of the sound *i*. How is the unlucky foreigner to guess the pronunciation of *indict*, *sign*, *buy*, *aisle*, *choir?* There are seven or eight ways of pronouncing *ough*. This is an argument for some sort of phonetic spelling which would stereotype the existing pronunciation and remove stumbling-blocks from the path of the intelligent foreigner.

But what is the existing pronunciation? In America, as in England and Scotland, there are many dialects, and one cannot say offhand that one is right and another wrong. I have never heard English spoken more purely than at Boston, Massachusetts; after my first visit to America I was ashamed to think that I had sometimes made *figure* rhyme with *nigger*. But I should be sorry to see the New York dialect made authoritative. I should regret the disappearance of Lowland Scots, but I cannot pretend to admire the speech of Aberdonians.

The Yorkshire and Devonshire dialects are too good to lose, but the State schools will probably destroy them. Besides this, the pronunciation of some words is changing even now. I used to be taught that only Cockneys sounded the *h* in *humour;* now the omission of the aspirate in this word is becoming an aristocratic peculiarity like the obsolete *yaller*, *brasslet*, *goold*, *cowcumber*, and *Haryot*. *Di'mond* is, I think, disappearing from West End drawing-rooms, and our daughters will probably call themselves *gurls*, a pronunciation which is still considered "middle class."

A standardised pronunciation would rule out certain degradations of vowel sounds, which are very common. All unaccented syllables tend to coalesce in an -*er* sound. A clerical precision in speech might preach a sermon from the text: "Do not *err*, my beloved brethren." It is said that some schoolchildren spell *to* as *ter*, which is the way they pronounce it. Even grown-up people sometimes make the same mistake. A man was taken to a hospital, and put to bed. The doctor, finding not much the matter with him, gave him a harmless mixture, to be taken "three times a day," and put up at the foot of his bed a Latin prescription ending with *ter die*. The patient, wishing to know the worst, took a furtive glance at what the doctor had written, and to his horror read, as he thought, his death warrant. Congratulating himself that it was not yet too late to escape from his assassins, he skipped out of bed and made a bolt for it.

The "Myth of Er," as a Platonist might call it, came from Harrow, and has spread to all who play "Rugger" and "Soccer."

I have heard *chune*, for *tune*, and even *taown*, from young women who ought to know better. Mispronunciation is curiously infectious: if children are sent for a few months to a rustic day school, as my daughters were during the air raids, they will pick up a rich provincial dialect.

In some ways, however, I think we now pronounce more carefully. In the eighteenth century the capital of England was called Lunnon; and Mr. Gladstone to the end called the late lamented British Constitution the *Constitootion*.

In an old-fashioned English grammar there appears (shocking to relate), among pairs of "words which are pronounced alike but spelt differently, *Indian* and *engine* ("injun!"). The German schools, before the war, industriously taught an ultra-Cockney dialect of English, convinced that this was to be the pronunciation of the future.

The Commission will have to deal carefully with national peculiarities; but they will hardly give their blessing to Australians who wish to call their country "Strylia." And will they sanction the Americanisms *dullicate*, *cornfidential*, and *tellaphone?* (The Americans say there are three rapid ways of disseminating information; tellagraph, tellaphone, and tell a woman.) The old pronunciation of certain towns like Shrewsbury, Derby, and Hertford is worth preserving, and is in danger.

So much for pronunciation. In dealing with the use of words, I hope the Commission will be firm with such phrases as "time and again," and "back of," which show signs of wishing to cross the Atlantic. Warnings should be given to young practitioners not to confound *eliminate* and *elicit*, like the cricket reporter who wrote: "The elevation of the century eliminated a cheer from the crowd"; or *predicate* and *predict* (even Mr. Thomas Hardy once committed this atrocity); and not to use "meticulous," or "of that ilk," without knowing the meanings. "Meticulous" is an unnecessary equivalent of "timid," and "of that ilk" means "of that same." "Macleod of that ilk" is only another way of saying "Macleod of Macleod."

A very common blunder is in the use of the participle: "Mr. B. addressed the House for two hours, when, being fatigued by his exertions, the House adjourned till the following day." The House was very probably fatigued, but the writer did not mean to say so.

It is too late to plead for the idiomatic distinction between the subjective and objective genitive; though I maintain that we ought to say "Mr. Brown's butler," but "the murderer of Mr. Brown," unless we mean that Mr. Brown keeps a murderer in his pay.

"Without" for "unless," and "like" for "as," are very common blunders.

Mistakes in arranging the order of words sometimes lead to ludicrous statements. A municipal overseer wrote "Paid to a woman whose husband was drowned by order of the vestry under London Bridge, one guinea." And there is a tombstone (in Ireland, naturally) which bears the pathetic inscription: "Erected to the memory of John Phillips accidentally shot as a mark of affection by his brother."

We have a few writers who still take the utmost pains to write well, as Froude and Robert Louis Stevenson always did. Mr. Lowes Dickinson and Mr. W. H. Hudson are conspicuous examples. But as a rule the modern author does not give himself time; he is in too great a hurry to make money, for good writing is desperately slow work. Poets generally write good prose, because they are accustomed to slow composition.

It is to be hoped that we shall always have a few artists in words; otherwise we shall soon have an English language which will be as inferior to the English of the best writers as the Greek of Lucian is to the Greek of Plato. We have a glorious language, which, in the hands of Milton or Burke, is one of the grandest instruments of human speech; but, like everything else, it needs keeping in repair, especially in a hustling age when everyone reads and writes in a hurry.

English composition, both in prose and verse, ought to be an important part of all secondary education. The pupils enjoy it, and soon learn, under a good teacher, how to write their own language.

1924.

II
Political

I

WAR AND POPULATION

(I)

I DO not suppose that many of my readers share my hobby for vital statistics, but the effect of war on population is a subject which must interest everybody, and a comparison of the losses in the great wars of history is instructive.

As far as mere numbers go, losses by war, like losses by pestilence, are soon recovered from. If we look at a chart of the births and deaths in Germany for the two generations before the Great War we shall see that each war is marked by a peak in the line showing the death rate and a ravine in the line showing the birth rate. But the ravine is followed by a hump lasting two or more years, and making good the numbers lost. The Great War has been followed in this country by the lowest death rates ever known. Infant mortality especially has never been so low as it is now. I do not know the reason of this; but it is an interesting example of how nature abhors a vacuum. The empty chairs at her table are not allowed to remain vacant for long.

The mischief of war, from the racial point of view, is that it selects the best for destruction. We shall never know what we have lost by the deaths of many thousands of our noblest young men. Even in physique, the next generation will be impoverished. It seems to be established that the stature of the French nation was lowered by the Napoleonic wars; and I do not think that the Americans have ever fully recovered from the Civil War of 1861–1865, in which over 600,000 perished out of a total population of 27 millions. The numerical loss was made good by immigrants of a type somewhat inferior to the splendid descendants of the English and Dutch colonists.

There have, however, been instances where war has been so destructive that a nation has either never recovered from it, or only after a long time. The Germans have often said that it took them more than a century to recover from the Thirty Years' War, in which more than half the population of Germany—some have even said two-thirds—were swept away. The most murderous of all modern wars was in South America, when the

Paraguayans fell foul of three more powerful neighbours. Nearly all the adult males were killed; the few survivors were kept by the women—to put it plainly, for stud purposes.

But as a rule, the effects of war are permanent only if the economic fabric of a country has been so disorganised that it cannot support anything like its former population. Loss of trade, or internal disorder, may have this effect. It is not yet certain whether Great Britain will be able in the future to find work for all its 48 million inhabitants.

To this we should perhaps add another possible cause of decay—loss of heart and of the will to live, as the result of foreign conquest. The Guanches of the Canaries are said to have died out from mere despair. Some of the South Sea Islands began to lose population as soon as the white man came; very few children are now born in the Marquesas Islands, though the race is physically a very fine one. The Maoris at one time seemed to be following the same path to extinction, but in this case the decay has happily been arrested.

Wars in antiquity were sometimes very sanguinary, but no reliance can be placed on the figures recorded by ancient historians. The Oriental likes high totals, but he seldom takes the trouble to count. Few now credit some of the enormous numbers given in the Old Testament, or Herodotus' estimate of the army of Xerxes. It is not impossible that Cæsar slaughtered nearly a million Gauls and Germans; the Romans several times exterminated large migratory tribes who were trying to invade the empire, and they do not seem to have spared the non-combatants in the horde.

When the Western Empire broke up, Europe sank into a horrible condition; constant wars and devastations destroyed civilisation in the West. Pope Gregory I (600 A.D.) declares that "the cities are in ruins, the country depopulated, the land turned into a desert. No husbandman is left in the fields, and almost no inhabitant in the cities; the small remnant of the human race is daily and ceaselessly tormented. If we still delight in such a world, we must love wounds, not joys." This appalling state of things continued for centuries. Luchaire's admirable book on France under Philippe Auguste presents a picture hardly less sombre than that of Pope Gregory. The whole country was the scene of constant war, massacre and pillage.

And what brought this purgatory of humanity to an end? Mainly, the art of fortification. "By 1300," says Professor Oman, "the defensive had obtained an almost complete mastery over the offensive, so that famine was the only certain weapon

in siegecraft." A century later, the only warfare
that was not too costly to pay consisted of plunder-
ing raids by small forces, like the campaigns of
Henry V in France. This victory of the defensive
over the offensive saved civilisation. How many of
us have reflected on the frightful danger to the future
of humanity contained in the discovery, during the
Great War, that no town can any longer be defended?
To me it seems that this terrible discovery may
herald a return to the Dark Ages, unless the nations
agree to make an end of war. It is the most sinister fact that has emerged from those disastrous
four years.

The most murderous wars of the Middle Ages
were those waged by the Huns and Tartars. Readers of Gibbon will remember the exploits of Genghiz Khan and Timour, and the pyramids of skulls
which they built to mark the sites of the towns
which they had destroyed. These mounted nomads
destroyed everything and created nothing; they
were an unmitigated curse to humanity. If Europe
had been all flat plains, like Russia and Hungary,
civilisation would probably have been finally extirpated by these savages, and the Mongolian type of
countenance would be prevalent to the shores of
the Atlantic.

During the century before the Reformation armies were usually small, and the loss of life in war was moderate. But the Battle of Towton, which decided the Wars of the Roses, was an exception. Thirty thousand Englishmen lay dead on the moor when that struggle was ended. This figure seems to me almost incredible; but it was the most sanguinary battle ever fought on English soil.

The Wars of Religion introduced a new ferocity into military and political history. The depopulation of Germany has already been mentioned, and wherever the Spaniards ruled, savage persecutions destroyed as many lives as the sword. Grotius says that in the Netherlands alone, and in the single reign of Charles V, 100,000 persons were put to death for their religion. Over 30,000 were burnt alive by the Spanish Inquisition. At the sack of Magdeburg 20,000 non-combatants were massacred.

During the 18th century war was becoming steadily more humane, and we read of no horrors like these. Nor were there many atrocities in the long wars with Napoleon. The numbers killed by the French revolutionists will never be accurately known, but they were not very large, judging by our terrible modern standards. The total loss of life in the great war of a hundred years ago has been variously estimated. Taine says: "Between 1804 and 1815 Napoleon sent to their doom more than

1,700,000 Frenchmen, to whom must be added probably two millions killed by him under the name of allies or enemies." These figures do not include the battles previous to 1804, and perhaps not deaths from disease. They are certainly far too low for the loss of life on both sides between 1790 and Waterloo. Other estimates vary between five and eight millions. Of the 600,000 men whom Napoleon led across the Niemen only a few thousand returned.

The next important war was that in the Crimea, 1853–1856. This war was fought under the rigorous climatic conditions of Southern Russia, and the winters were exceptionally severe, while on both sides the health of the soldiers were scandalously neglected. The English Secretary of War computed the total Russian loss at nearly half a million, of whom only a small fraction were killed in action. The French lost about 95,000 and the English a larger percentage of a smaller army.

This enormous wastage of men through sickness ceased in the war between France and Germany in 1870. Considering the number of hardly-fought battles, the loss of life on both sides sounds to us very small. The Germans lost about 30,000 killed, and 12,000 by disease; the losses of the French, apart from prisoners, were probably about the same. But the massacres in Paris during the suppression of the Commune doubled the butcher's bill. Some 20,000 Communists were shot by the Government troops.

Lastly, in the Russo-Japanese War, each side mobilised about a million men. Nearly a quarter of these on each side were casualties, or died of sickness; but I do not know what proportion of the wounded recovered.

In my next article I shall attempt to estimate the loss of life in the Great War, both direct and indirect.

1922.

II

WAR AND POPULATION

(II)

LAST week I collected from past history statistics of slaughter in war. The most devastating conflicts in modern times, since gunpowder made civilisation fairly safe from savage inroads, have been the so-called Wars of Religion. After Europe settled down into Protestantism and Catholicism, and neither party sought any longer to exterminate the other, warfare became more humane, until the new principle of nationality exacerbated the strife of peoples, and the pressure of population upon subsistence diminished the value of human life.

The recent Great War has surpassed all others in destructiveness; the loss of life by shell and bullet is only a small part of the slaughter caused directly or indirectly by the four years' struggle. In this article I shall attempt a rough estimate of the number of human beings who would have been alive if there had been no war, and who are now either dead or unborn.

Most of the belligerents have published reliable statements of their casualties. The proportion of killed to wounded is greater than in earlier wars because this was mainly an artillery war. It must be remembered that many names occur three or four times on the list of wounded. Disregarding for our present purpose the minor casualties, I find that the number of those who were killed in action or died of wounds in all parts of the world is nearly ten millions, and that the Allies lost nearly double as many men as the Central Powers. The largest contribution to the total is made by the Russians, who were driven like sheep to the slaughter, in some cases unarmed, and always insufficiently protected by artillery.

The next item to be considered is the decline in the number of births owing to the absence of husbands on military service. The Registrar-General estimates the loss at 600,000, but this is for England and Wales only, and he deducts from the deficiency during the war the surplus of births above the average in the year following demobilisation. As the birth rate rose to 29 per thousand in the first quarter of 1920, this makes a considerable difference. Without this deduction, and including

the whole British Empire, I estimate the loss of
population from the decline in births at a million.
In some other nations the birth rate fell during the
war even more than it did with us; I believe we
may reckon the total loss from this cause as from
twelve to fifteen millions.

The mortality from disease caused by the war is
very difficult to compute. For the first time in
the history of warfare the deaths of soldiers from
sickness, on the western front, were a quite insig-
ficant item in the mortality lists. When we consider that two huge armies occupied approximately
the same positions for years, and those positions
deep trenches in a heavily-manured country, the
absence of epidemics is the more extraordinary.

It was due partly to the strictness with which
sanitary rules were enforced, and still more to
inoculation. At the beginning of the war a certain society instituted an agitation against inoculation and inserted full page advertisements in
many respectable papers. I wrote indignant letters to two of the editors, and in one case received a
most courteous reply, promising that the advertisement should not appear again, and it did not. Two
of the worst scourges, enteric and tetanus, were
most successfully dealt with by inoculation.

In the east of Europe typhus and cholera made

great havoc; it was estimated that nearly one-third of the whole Serbian nation succumbed. But no accurate statistics are available.

The great epidemic of influenza may or may not have been caused, or greatly aggravated, by war conditions. It killed 100,000 persons in Great Britain, and seven or eight millions in the world at large. The mortality was extremely heavy in India, and few countries escaped the visitation.

We come next to famine and massacre, which cannot be separated, since one method of massacre is to drive the inhabitants of a district into some place where they must necessarily die of hunger. The Germans claim that our blockade caused the deaths of 750,000 Germans who, but for the blockade, would not have died. There is reason to think that this estimate is much exaggerated, but there is no doubt that the death rate in Germany and Austria was increased by the shortage of wholesome food.

In England the death rate from natural causes remained low through the war, except when influenza was raging. The number of civilians massacred, chiefly in Belgium, or killed by air raids and submarines, is not easy to estimate. The total is small compared with the enormous figures with which we have been dealing. Several thousands of

British merchant sailors were drowned, and about 1400 persons were killed in England by air-bombs.

The population of Russia is now estimated at 130 millions. Before the war (with a larger area) it was 180 millions. Probably some 30 millions of lives have been sacrificed to the Moloch of Communism. The birth rate of Russia, which before the war was at the barbaric rate of 44 per thousand, has fallen now by 40 per cent. It seems that even the moujik, little accustomed as he is to self-restraint, shrinks from the cruelty of bringing children into the world of Lenin and Trotsky.

The majority of the thirty millions have died of hunger and disease, and the mortality has naturally been greatest in the towns, where all industries have ceased, so that the inhabitants have nothing but waste-paper roubles to give in exchange for the food which the peasants refuse to part with. In many parts of Russia the peasants are better off than they were before the war. They grow enough food for their own families, and can procure manufactured articles, made before 1914, for a small handful of grain. The population of Petrograd, which in 1914 was 2,200,000, has now dwindled to about 650,000.

But direct massacre has played a large part in the depopulation of Russia. The Paris *Gaulois* a short

time ago published the reports of the notorious
"Extraordinary Commission" which had been
printed in the Soviet newspapers. Since October,
1917, when the Bolshevists came into power, executions in Russia numbered:—

Bishops	28	Constabulary	48,500
Priests	1,215	Landowners	12,950
Professors and teachers	6,775	Intelligentsia and	
Doctors	8,800	Middle-class	355,350
Army officers	54,000	Peasants	815,100
Soldiers	260,000		
Police officers	10,000		
			1,572,718

All these have been butchered in cold blood by
the revolutionary tribunals. When we remember
that the massacres have continued since this list
was drawn up, and that it does not include other
murders, of which there have been an enormous
number, it will be a moderate estimate to say that
the Communists have slaughtered two millions of
their fellow-citizens, including nearly all those who
might have contributed to the re-establishment of
civilised conditions in that unfortunate country.
Let those who have blamed me for doubting the
actuality (not the possibility) of moral progress say
whether past history records anything approaching
the scale of these horrors.

It is no wonder that the Bolshevists express sympathy with the Turks, for the Turks are their equals in the theory and practice of wholesale butchery. The Armenian nation has been almost extirpated, and the "Greeks" of Asia Minor, who, it will be remembered, are not immigrants from European Greece, but the descendants of the subjects of the East-Roman Empire, conquered by the Turks in the Middle Ages, have not fared much better.

It is only possible to guess at the numbers who have been slaughtered by the Turks or driven from their homes to perish from hunger. From such figures as are available I should say that the total cannot be less than two millions, and may be considerably more. The Christian nations of the Balkans have not been much less ruthless.

These figures speak for themselves, though in the presence of so awful a calamity the imagination fails to realise all that they mean. There has been nothing like it in history; and it is a melancholy reflection that this orgy of murder should have come at the end of a century of comparative peace and orderly progress.

We have to reconsider many things which we formerly took for granted. Our minds travel back to the happy and prosperous age of the Antonines, when civilisation seemed so secure, and when humane philosophies and legislation were so much in fashion. That period ended in universal chaos and the destruction of culture; and it was only after about seven hundred years that the foundations of a new civilisation were laid.

Is the world to be a second time resolved into a mutual suicide club; or will wiser counsels prevail? I hope for the best, and am not despondent; but let us all realise what is involved in the success or failure of the good men and women who are labouring to heal the wounds of the war, and to set the civilised world once more on a sound basis of co-operation and security.

1922.

III

THE WAR LOSSES

A FEW months ago I attempted to estimate the loss of life caused by the Great War, and to compare it with other wars in the past. I have always been fond of statistics, and the figures at which I arrived were very near the truth. But the Carnegie Research Committee has now issued a far more detailed survey, and the results are so interesting that a *résumé* of their findings may be welcome to my readers.

I called attention to one fact of great importance. Although the number of men killed in action in the Great War far exceeded all previous records, the mortality from disease was so much less than in all earlier wars that the proportion of lives lost to the number of soldiers mobilised was not very large. I am now in a position to substantiate this statement.

In the Seven Years' War (1756–1763) the Austrians lost 32,000 killed and 93,400 by wounds and

disease. The Prussians began the war with 126,000
men, and Frederick the Great estimated that
180,000 had lost their lives before the end of it.
Of 80,000 Russians who entered Poland in 1757, less
than half remained alive in the autumn of that
year. Most of these losses were due to disease.

The losses in the Napoleonic wars are difficult
to calculate, partly because Napoleon, who invented the phrase, "*Mentir comme un bulletin,*"
did his best to justify the proverb. At Eylau, where
he lost 23,150 men, he only owned to 1,900 killed and
5,700 wounded. The total French losses during the
wars (excluding foreign conscripts), were probably about two million killed or died of disease.
There is, unfortunately, no separate computation
of the losses from sickness.

But the figures for the British Navy are very instructive. During the 20 years when we were at
war, between 1793 and 1815, 6,663 sailors were
killed by the enemy, 13,621 were drowned or killed
in shipwrecks or fires, and 72,102 died of disease.
For the British Army in the same period 25,569
were killed or died of wounds, 193,851 died of disease. We lost more than seven times as many
men by sickness as by the fire of the enemy.

Napoleon carried about 600,000 men, including
a large proportion of foreign conscripts, into Russia

in 1812. Only a few thousand returned in a condition to carry arms. At Vilna 25,000 out of 30,000 prisoners died of typhus.

The Russian army which invaded Turkey in 1828 was almost exterminated by disease; scurvy in particular caused great ravages.

In the Crimean War, where the arrangements were notoriously scandalous, we lost only 4,602 men by wounds, and 17,580 by disease. The French lost 20,240 by wounds and 75,375 by disease. Eleven thousand Frenchmen died of cholera. The Austrian army of 283,000 men, who did not fight at all, lost 35,000 from disease.

In the American Civil War (1861–1865), the Northern States lost 110,000 killed and 224,586 from disease; but these figures are slightly reduced by other authorities. The South lost about 120,000 from disease. In the prison camps of the South the mortality was nearly 30 per cent. Even in the Seven Weeks' War (1866), the Prussians lost over 6,000 by cholera and other diseases.

In the Franco-German War of 1870 we find for the first time that more men were killed in action or died of wounds than from disease; but typhus and typhoid were both very fatal.

The Russians in 1877, fighting the Turks, lost 30,000 killed and 80,000 by disease. Great Britain in the Boer War lost only 7,534 killed and 14,382 by disease. In the Russo-Japanese War the effects of modern methods are clearly shown; in both armies the losses by disease were much less than the fatal casualties.

In the Great War, the loss by sickness is known to have been relatively insignificant, except in the East; but unfortunately no figures are given, except for Italy.

The total casualties in the Great War are very variously calculated. Comparing one estimate with another, the losses of life among the various belligerents were, in round numbers:—Russia, 1,700,000 killed and 1,300,000 died of disease; Germany, 2,000,000; France, 1,400,000; British Empire, 950,-000; Austria, a million and a half (including heavy losses by disease); Italy, nearly half a million; Turkey, perhaps 350,000; America, between 50,000 and 100,000. The losses of the Balkan States were relatively enormous. Mr. Vedel Petersen, the Danish statistician, says: "The total number of military persons killed and died must lie between ten and eleven millions, but Russia's losses are not known and presumably never will be."

Another very interesting calculation is of the number of births which the war prevented. The same authority estimates these as follows:—Great

Political

Britain, about 600,000; France, about a million (this is curious, for the French gave all married men periodical leave, in order to obviate this result); Italy, 1,290,000; Germany, nearly three millions; Austria, about the same. These figures bear out my statement that the loss of population due to the separation of husbands and wives was slightly greater than the fatal war casualties, but the number here given for Great Britain seems to me too low.

The loss of life among civilians, due to the war, is difficult to calculate. It is not certain whether the influenza epidemic of 1918, which is said to have killed some eight million people all over the world, and which caused 112,000 deaths (far more than any visitation of cholera) in Great Britain alone, would have occurred if there had been no war. Probably it would at any rate have been far less destructive. As far as I can make out from Mr. Vedel Petersen's figures, though he does not say so explicitly, the epidemic spared only two countries in Europe—Germany and Austria!

The statistics of civilian mortality in Germany in my opinion disprove the statement made frequently in Germany that our blockade caused the deaths of 750,000 non-combatants in that country. The increase in civilian deaths was not markedly great till the last year of the war, which was the influenza year, and the average infant mortality was actually much less in the first three and a half years of the war than in the years preceding 1914. This improvement in infant mortality was also observed in England, and was attributed in part to the diminution of drunkenness on Saturday nights!

It is also quite untrue that the children of Vienna "died like flies," as some speakers for the "Save the Children Fund" asserted. There was undoubtedly great privation, and the efforts of the Fund to relieve it were amply justified, but why cannot good people be content to speak the truth?

The following statement about Cologne is rather appalling. "Before the war there were 45.2 illegitimate for every 100 legitimate births, whereas during the war the proportion fell to 40.2." In England and Wales the proportion of illegitimate births was between 4 and 5 per thousand; in 1918 it unfortunately rose to 6.3 per thousand.

Terrible as these war statistics are, the destruction of life is not to be compared with the depopulation of Germany during the thirty years' war of the seventeenth century, when the population of Bohemia was reduced from four million to 800,000, and the Palatinate was almost denuded of inhabitants.   The Tai-ping rebellion in China is the only modern war which produced horrors comparable to this, unless we include the judicial massacres by the Bolshevists.

Will mankind ever determine to put an end to these colossal follies and crimes?   The strangest thing is that they are not willed by anybody, and yet they happen.   As Professor Dumas of Lausanne says in this book: "Although the instinct of self-preservation is very strong, war gives rise to forces strong enough to hold it in check, with the result that we find millions of men ready to shed their blood in order that their comrades may pillage a town and violate its women, or in order that their compatriots may speak the language they love, profess the faith they believe right, and obey only their chosen leaders."   The motives, in fact, range from the noblest to the basest in human nature.

1922.

IV

AMBASSADOR PAGE'S LETTERS

(I)

THOSE who had the privilege of knowing personally Mr. Walter Page, while he was American Ambassador in England, will read with the keenest interest the two volumes of his letters which have just been published. Mr. Page was in manner and appearance very unlike the typical diplomat. He was just a fine specimen of the American gentleman, evidently shrewd and capable, straightforward and honest—a man to be trusted.

His wife, who survives him, made no attempt to play the great lady. She was simple, warm-hearted, and kindly to her English friends.

The Embassy was a delightful house to visit. I shall not forget a dinner-party there a few weeks before the war, when we met the Lichnowskys, who, by the way, kept us all waiting a good half-hour in the drawing-room.

Poor Prince Lichnowsky! We now know why this Anglophil Polish nobleman was chosen to represent Germany in London in 1914. One of our diplomats, who had watched the machinations of Germany on the Continent, and had no doubt what was coming, wrote, when he heard of the appointment, "*This is the anæsthetic before the operation.*" Lichnowsky did not understand the part which had been assigned to him, but there were others in London, to do the unavowed and unavowable work. This was an old trick of the German Government.

Mr. Page is now revealed as one of the best friends England ever had. It seems really providential that an unfriendly President—for there is no doubt that Mr. Wilson disliked this country, and did all he could to keep America out of the war—should have sent to the London Embassy the one man whose heart was set on binding the two nations together in a firm friendship. For this he laboured strenuously and unceasingly all the time he was among us. For this he sacrificed his life, dying of overwork at the age of sixty-three, just before the end of the Great War. He deserves to be gratefully remembered by all future generations of Englishmen, and it is to be hoped that our historians will do him justice.

The English Embassy has long been considered

the blue ribbon of the American Diplomatic Service, and one of the most honourable posts open to a
citizen of the United States. It has been held by a
series of distinguished men, who have been welcomed
in this country for their brilliant intellectual gifts
and for their happy knack of making excellent
speeches. A tradition has been created which
must task the energies of the ablest Ambassador to
keep up. And yet the great Republic put every
kind of difficulty in the way of its representatives.
Alone among the nations represented in England
by Ambassadors, America had no residence for
its envoy. How great was the inconvenience thus
caused to a new Ambassador Mr. Page's letters
prove.

Nor was this all. Mr. Page soon discovered that
while the American nation was held in honour and
esteem by the British people, the American Government was regarded, and not unreasonably, with
resentment, as an unfriendly body of men, always
ready to pick a quarrel, and positively enjoying any
affront that could be offered to Great Britain. Mr.
Page himself was shocked at the habitual rudeness
of Washington. The usual tone of American dis-
patches to this country was that of a lawyer writing
to a shady individual who is trying to swindle his
respectable client. Sometimes the messages were

so offensive that the Ambassador could not present them, for fear that even the long-suffering Foreign Office might refuse to receive them. This rudeness was reserved for Great Britain; even after the war began, Washington observed the forms of diplomatic courtesy in corresponding with Germany.

This, of course, gave huge satisfaction to the Irish Americans, whose votes are an important consideration, especially to the Democratic Party. The Ambassador was, fortunately, not required to insult his hosts; but in 1895 the House of Representatives formally censured Ambassador Bayard for a few civil words about England, spoken at a public banquet.

Such were the difficulties with which Mr. Page had to cope. He had always liked the English, though his approbation was tempered by a whole bundle of American prejudices. But at first he was conscious of no difference between the view of President Wilson and his own.

It is most interesting to observe the increasing warmth of his championship of our countrymen. It was based on two foundations—first, he came to realise more and more the sterling qualities of the English race; and, second, he had not the slightest doubt from the first that the Great War was no struggle between predatory empires for loot and predominance, but a plain matter of right and wrong, in which the Allies were in the right and Germany in the wrong.

The political importance of these letters will be considered in a second paper. They are of great value at a time when the German propaganda is being taken up by English apologists for their country's foes, one of whom, and he the cleverest, has unhappily been returned to the House of Commons by a northern constituency. To-day I wish to call attention to Mr. Page's judgments of our national character and institutions.

To take the less agreeable part of his comments first, Mr. Page is a thorough American in his attitude to European institutions, which he criticises with a curious *naïveté*. He is unable to think of any reason why we preserve manners and customs which link the present with the past, except that we are too stupid to abolish them. A king, for instance, is a medieval survival, who is always ridiculous and generally wicked. (Happily, he makes a hearty exception in favour of King George.)

He offers incense to the American fetish Democracy in almost every letter. "There is no security in any part of the world where people cannot think of a government without a king, and never will be. You cannot conceive of a democracy that will unprovoked set out on a career of conquest." After reading such sentences as these, one can only gasp, and wonder whether the Americans are only praying to their national god, or whether they are hypocrites. History, and not least American history, tells a very different story. A Mexican, a Spaniard, a Filipino, or a Japanese, would have something to say about the aversion of democracies to wars of conquest. This obsession, which even several years in England could not dispel from so open-minded and intelligent a man as Walter Page, illustrates one of the difficulties in Anglo-American relations. There is a great deal to be said for democracy, but to worship it is a provincialism, and quite out of date.

He also speaks several times of our arrogance, and gives us, in return, some choice examples of American modesty. "What are we going to do with the leadership of the world when it falls into our hands? How can we use the English for the highest uses of democracy?" "The English and the whole English world are ours, if we have the courtesy to take them—Fleet and trade and all." "It will fall to us to loose and set free the British, and a Briton set free is an American." "We can lead the British and French and develop their whole people."

It is needless to say that Mr. Page wishes to

take over our affairs entirely for our good, and to turn us into good Americans in the gentlest and kindest manner. But what terrible difficulties there may be in the future with this self-complacent and self-righteous nation, which is as convinced as the Germans were in 1914 that their *Kultur* is the only civilisation worth having, and that they cannot do another people a better service than by abolishing its customs and traditions and turning English and French towns into duplicates of *Main Street?*

It is a pleasure to turn to Mr. Page's generous words about the conduct of our people during the war.

"The world never saw a finer lot of men than the best of their ruling class. I meet such men everywhere—gently bred, high-minded, physically fit, intellectually cultivated, patriotic. I can't see that the race is breaking down or giving out. They write and speak and play cricket and govern and fight as well as they have ever done."

"Another conclusion that is confirmed the more you see of English life is their high art of living. They have gentleness, cultivation, the best manners in the world; and they are genuine."

"Not a tear have I seen yet" he says again. "You guess at their grief only by their reticence. It isn't an accident that these people own a fifth of the world. Utterly unwarlike, they outlast anybody else when war comes. You don't get a sense of fighting here, only of endurance and high resolve."

"The heroism, the generosity, the endurance and self-restraint and courtesy of these people would melt a pyramid to tears."

"There never was such a race. It is the fashion in the United States to say that the British are not doing their share. There never was a greater slander. All the old stories of bravery from Homer down are outdone every day by these people. When the real trial comes they don't flinch, and (except the thoroughbred American) there are no such men in the world."

1922.

V

AMBASSADOR PAGE'S LETTERS

(II)

MR. PAGE'S letters, as I said in my article of last week, throw a flood of light on the relations of Great Britain and America during the Great War. We did not realise at the time what dangerous rocks there were through which Sir Edward Grey and the American Ambassador in London piloted the ship. In 1914 there was even a possibility that the United States Government might repeat the crime of 1812, and stab us in the back while we were fighting for our existence and for the liberties of Europe.

All danger of this disaster, for which the American people would have repented bitterly when it was too late, was averted by the tact of our Foreign Secretary and Mr. Page. When at last American public opinion obliged the President to come to the help of the Allies, Mr. Page did another great service by forcing his Government to realise that the submarine menace was far more serious than they were willing to believe. He lived just long enough to hear of the fine exploits of the American troops on the Western front, but he did not see the final victory of the Allies.

Hardly less important are the sidelights which this book casts on the causes of the war, and on the mentality of the different belligerents. This evidence is especially valuable now, when the Germans are sedulously cultivating an entirely untrue legend, exonerating themselves and inculpating the Entente Powers.

The first testimony is the mission of Colonel House (or Mr. House as he prefers to be called) to Germany in May, 1914. This very able American publicist went to Berlin simply in the cause of peace. Page was not hopeful, but encouraged him to go. And this is what he found. Von Tirpitz consumed a large part of the time which House spent with him in denouncing England and all its works. He did not conceal his opposition to any peace propaganda. Even worse than the unsympathetic attitude of the German Ministers was the general atmosphere of Berlin. The military oligarchy was in absolute control, and the populace was already possessed with the war fever. Every able-bodied man in Berlin seemed to be practising rifle-shooting.

The Emperor wished to see Mr. House, but every obstacle was placed in the way of a private interview. When at last they met, the Kaiser said, probably sincerely, that he did not wish for war, but he spent most of the time talking about the Yellow Peril, which, as I found when I was in Berlin two or three years before, was very much on the brain of the official class. House returned in a state of consternation at the spirit which he found everywhere in Germany. "I feel," he said, "as though I had been living near a mighty electric dynamo. The whole of Germany is charged with electricity. Everybody's nerves are tense. It needs only a spark to set the whole thing off." The spark came a fortnight later.

House went next to Paris, where he found the French engrossed with their domestic troubles, and not thinking of war at all. England, in the same way, he found entirely preoccupied with Ulster and the Suffragettes. He talked to Asquith, Grey and Lloyd George, but "none of these men apprehended an immediate war." They had complete confidence in Lichnowsky and Bethmann Hollweg.

Then came the "grand smash." Mr. Page gives us vivid pictures of the behaviour of the chief men whom he saw in London. The King, deeply moved, cried, "My God, Mr. Page, what else could we do?"

Mensdorff, the popular Austrian Ambassador, shut himself up in his Embassy, weeping and wailing, and only ejaculating, "My dear colleague! My dear colleague!" Lichnowsky, who had not slept for several nights, was like a man demented. "He came down in his pyjamas, a crazy man." Sir Edward Grey was quiet and restrained. He explained to Page that the neutrality of Belgium was secured by treaty; that Germany was a signatory power to the treaty; that civilisation rests upon such solemn compacts; that the action of Germany meant the end of the independence of Belgium; and that Germany would not be content without seizing Holland and Denmark too. "England would be for ever contemptible if it should sit by and see this treaty violated."

And then his eyes filled with tears, and he added: "Thus the efforts of a lifetime go for nothing. I feel like a man who has wasted his life."

A very significant document is a long letter from the wife of a German merchant at Bremen. This good lady merely reflects the talk that she had heard from her husband and his friends. She begins by taunting England with having made no sacrifice for political power—with having, in a word, no army ready for war. And so "our officers are absolutely confident that they will land ten army corps in England before Christmas. They mean to destroy. Birmingham, Leeds, Bradford, Newcastle, Sheffield, Northampton are to be wiped out and the men killed. The fact that Great Britain is to be a Reichsland will involve the destruction of its inhabitants, to enable Germans to be planted in the country in their place. . . . But England is only a stepping-stone. From Liverpool, Queenstown, Glasgow, Belfast, we shall reach out across the ocean. Within a year Germany will have seized the new canal and proclaimed its defiance of the great Monroe Doctrine. The Americans are a cowardly nation." And so on.

This was, in truth, the temper in which Germany began the war. The Germans meant to conquer the world, and in doing so to perpetrate massacres of non-combatants on a scale which would throw the exploits of Attila, Genghiz Khan, and Timour into the shade. It was a kind of maniacal exaltation, affecting a large part of the population. Probably the Kaiser and his Ministers would have been quite unable to keep down the demon which their systematic poisoning of the public mind had raised. The Kaiser, if he had stood out against the war party, would have been promptly deposed.

And now, as I know by several letters from strangers in Germany, this strange people entirely denies that it ever wished for war with anybody. The writers seem to have absolutely forgotten their fit of homicidal mania. I am sure they are not consciously lying; their tone is one of injured innocence and of intense indignation at the injustice which the world has done them. They have in fact recovered their sanity, and have honestly forgotten what they said and did during the fit of delirium. I am afraid it would be easy to find utterances by Englishmen and Frenchmen, hardly less horrible than the letter of the lady of Bremen. But there was nothing of the kind here *before* the war broke out.

The evidence in this book is thus extremely valuable. I have been well abused for urging that we should put away our war mentality, and think only of the reconstruction of Europe, on which our trade and employment for our population depend. We have an honourable tradition against keeping up animosity against an enemy, and I hope we shall always maintain it.

But it is one thing to plead for Christianity and common sense; it is quite another thing to declare, in the teeth of the evidence, that the Germans were not the aggressors in the late war. This is what some of our writers are doing. For some strange reason, such arguments seem to be popular with the Labour Party,

both here and abroad.   I have before me a copy of
the French *Hansard*, a highly amusing report of a
debate on war responsibility in the French Chamber.
The members of the "extreme left" use much the
same language as our Socialists, though such ex-
clamations as "Taisez-vous, profiteur!" would be
hardly in order in our Parliament.   Every one to his
taste; if these gentlemen like to champion their
country's enemies, there is no more to be said.

But the verdict of impartial history is not in doubt.
The Germans are condemned by such unimpeachable
testimony as that which we find in Ambassador
Page's correspondence.

1922.

VI

AMERICA IN THE GREAT WAR

I AM glad Mr. Kipling has been able to repudiate the attack upon America put into his mouth by a New York paper. Unfairness to America should be avoided by every loyal Englishman, and Mr. Kipling, as well as being a great poet and a great prose writer, is also a great patriot. The so-called interview with him would have done us great mischief if it had been taken in America as representing Great Britain's thought. For it was very unfair to America. The assumption seemed to be that the Great War was a crusade in which every self-respecting nation ought to have joined at once.

The truth is that it began as a quarrel between the Teuton and the Slav, and that we came in because we could not afford to see an arrogant and ambitious military Power dominating the whole Continent of Europe. As Mr. Asquith said in August, 1914, "if we had kept out we should have been left without a friend in the world," marked out as the next victim.

But America was not threatened at all in the same way. A German victory would certainly have been highly inconvenient for the United States. It would have compelled the Americans to militarise themselves, and to be prepared for a possible war in South America in defence of the Monroe doctrine. But they thought that the Allies could tackle Germany without their help, and being neither more nor less selfish than other people, they preferred to sell munitions and lend money, till the sudden collapse of Russia obliged them to intervene in a hurry. Considering their tradition of not meddling with European politics, I do not see how we could expect them to act otherwise.

There is one question which Englishmen seldom ask themselves, although the answer would clear up many historical and political problems from the battle of Waterloo to our own day. The question is this. Why did the world acquiesce so readily in the expansion of the British Empire? Why did the other great Powers allow us to snap up not only unconsidered trifles in the tropics, but such enormous prizes as Australia, New Zealand, and South Africa?

These annexations were made, of course, in virtue of our maritime supremacy. But why was this supremacy never challenged? Why were there no coalitions against us?

It seems to me that we were left unmolested in consideration of an unwritten understanding in which there were three clauses: first, we were to keep our army so small that it could not be a threat to any Continental Power; second, we were not to exclude foreign trade by tariffs; third, we were not to make alliances with any of the great military Powers of Europe.

So long as these unwritten terms were observed, our naval supremacy was an enormous advantage to civilisation. We prevented the possibility of land and sea power being united in the hands of any one nation. We protected the young nations beyond the seas, including the United States, from the danger of attack; for no coalition against America could be formed without our consent. We procured for the civilised world a century of comparative peace, and made possible the unexampled progress of humanity in wealth and population which was the salient feature of the nineteenth century.

It was thus the interest of the whole world that our naval supremacy should continue. The very possibility of the trident being grasped by Germany, the possessor of the strongest army, was profoundly unwelcome to almost every other nation. It was this,

I believe, more than any other cause, which led to the vast coalition against Germany in the late war. The Germans, if they had thought it worth while to look through the eyes of others, might have predicted that the world would not tolerate a German victory. Their success would have menaced the security of almost every nation in the world. The fate of Germany was sealed by the Kaiser's foolish speech, "The trident must be in our hands."

But with the German navy under the waves at Scapa Flow American interest in the European tangle ceased. The United States is now invulnerable. No Power or combination of Powers could attack it, and it possesses all the gold of the world. Its only potential rival is, unfortunately, this country.

Accordingly the American Government is consulting its own interest by forgiving other nations their debts, which it could never recover, and by pressing us for repayment of the huge loan to France to which we were foolish enough to put our names. By so doing the Americans can lay us under a tribute which will make it impossible for us to challenge the naval supremacy which has now passed into their hands.

Nobody could pretend that this action is generous or friendly. But why should we expect a higher standard of conduct from them than from the French, or the Germans, or the Russians? We have to judge all other nations by the prevailing standard of international morality; that is to say, by the lowest standard on which human beings ever act deliberately. It is no use complaining; we must make the best of a bad business.

We can, however, help our country by trying to remove from the minds of Americans the special antipathy to England which is almost a tradition on the other side of the Atlantic.

In doing this we shall be supporting a noble body of Americans, the best part of the nation, who are thoroughly friendly to us, and who are working hard to establish real bonds of sympathy between the two countries. Some of these men are friends of my own; with others I have been in correspondence. They are conducting an uphill fight against prejudice and animosity, and I think they are gaining ground.

It is at present hopeless to make an American realise the truth about Ireland, but I have read many recent American utterances about England which show real affection and appreciation—utterances which do one's heart good.

The ties which bind the two nations together— our common language, literature, and institutions— must in the long run prove far stronger than the

temporary and almost accidental causes of estrange-
ment—the dim memories of the War of Independence, the very unfair schoolbooks from which American children learn their history, and the malice of
certain immigrants and their descendants, who
must in time be absorbed in the mass of American nationals, and drop their senseless inherited
vendettas.

The Americans have put a stop to promiscuous
immigration, so that the Americans of the future will
in the main be the descendants of the present inhabitants.   Of these the majority are either of British
descent or capable of assimilating Anglo-Saxon civilisation.   There will be far more interchange of ideas
between them and us than with any other European country.   With tact and patience on our
side the bad old tradition ought to disappear by
degrees.

So far as I can see, everything points to this country being in the future an Oceanic rather than a
European Power.   We also are disposed to wash our
hands of European quarrels, now that our danger
from Germany has, for the time being, passed away.
Every year makes the Dominions a more important
part of the British nation.   The time is not far distant when they will actually outnumber us.   They
may, I think, be a valuable intermediary in our re-

lations with America, sharing, as they do, many of the characteristics of young and hopeful democracies.

In the far future an English-speaking League is not unthinkable. Let us do what we can to bring it nearer.

1922.

VII

AMERICAN CHARACTER

WHEN I was last in Berlin, two years before the war, I said to my host: "Europe will lead the world about fifty years more, after which the supremacy will pass to the United States. But if Europe goes to war, the Americans will take the sceptre and the trident at once, and neither you nor we will ever recover them." My prediction has come true, and consequently America is now by far the most interesting country in the world. The Americans are our masters.

I have been reading again George Santayana's *Character and Opinion in the United States*. This ex-Professor of Harvard has been in England since the beginning of the war, so that he tells us nothing of any changes which may have come to American character in consequence of the world-struggle and of the enormous prosperity which it brought to the United States alone among the combatants. But his book is peculiarly interesting, because he views

American civilisation with a great detachment as well as with intimate knowledge. Such detachment would not be possible to a "hundred per cent. American," nor even to an Englishman; but it is possible to one who by descent belongs to the Latin countries. Professor Santayana is a Spaniard.

The Latin nations have an older civilisation than ours. Their ancestors were Romans, and they initiated the Renaissance. They are more sceptical, more logical, harder, and less sentimental than we are. They have studied the art of living more finely. For the Latin, the important matter is to like the right things—to get his values right. The Anglo-Saxon, he thinks, believes a great many things which cannot be known, and is content to leave his values in a state of chaos. For all his energy and practical success, he is at bottom a barbarian. He accumulates the means of fine living, and does not know what to do with them. He makes a great deal of money, and then gives it away—which the Latin never does! He is a fine fellow, no doubt; but the Latin does not envy him or wish to imitate him.

The interesting thing about Professor Santayana is that, while he feels all this, he has a sincere admiration for the Anglo-Saxon character, and understands England in particular very well. Our author finds the American character very uniform; on which I shall have something to say presently.   He lived, we must remember, in New England, the most conservative part of the country.   The New England tradition is Calvinistic.   Now Calvinism is the Christian form of Stoicism.   It arose in democratic and busy Geneva, while Lutheranism was flavoured partly bu the monkish training of Luther himself and partly by the agrarian and semi-feudal society in which it took root.   Calvin instituted the asceticism of hard work.   We serve God best by taking our place in civil life, and doing our business, whatever it is, thoroughly well.   We are to eschew superfluities, which take up time and distract attention.   The glory of God and the well-being of society are the only objects worth living for.   In this way Calvinism is responsible for that curious product, the modern business man.   No other form of Christianity has accepted with less reserve the social conditions of modern industrialism, or has felt so much at home in the bank, the shop, and the factory.   At the same time, it has always frowned upon the idle rich and the mere *rentier*.

Calvinism has flourished in Scotland, and still more in America, long after it decayed in England. It may still be studied in the United States, though its angles, and something more than angles, have been rubbed off.   It still inspires the ethical and even the devotional literature of that country. The Middle Ages made a business of religion; the American almost makes a religion of business. "Be Christians, and you will be successful," cried the Head of a great University to his students. This is a parody of a very intelligible conviction, which belongs to Calvinism. A man is confident that he is called to salvation; he sees his duty in carrying on and accelerating the movement of a vast, progressive society, and is sure that God and nature are working with him. Till lately his confidence in life has almost made the American think that the devil has forgotten America.

So we picture the typical American, healthy, clean-minded, and indomitably cheerful, springing from his bed in the morning, and, after a bath and deep-breathing exercises, to which he attaches great importance, praying that in the coming day he may be helpful to others, happy, strenuous, and successful. He asks himself no difficult questions; the proof of his religion is that it makes him a very efficient member of society. This kind of Christianity is so utterly unlike Catholicism that we may wonder what an American does when he joins the Church of Rome. But he is not at all embarrassed; he belongs to the biggest religion on earth, anyway; and America has three Cardinals.

It may be doubted whether America has yet produced a really indigenous and characteristic literature. The famous New England school—Emerson, Longfellow, and the rest, were among the most enviable of human beings, but their conception of life was, as Santayana says, "expurgated and barren." They demurely kept up with the times; but it was all a harvest of leaves. Walt Whitman, who was hailed in Europe as racy of the soil, was repudiated in America; his countrymen could not forgive his improprieties. The best among recent American novelists are, strangely enough, rather bitter and sad when they describe social life; a new feature and perhaps significant. Their most distinguished philosophers, James and Royce, are more amateurish than even our own, when compared with the Germans. Their incursions into metaphysics are of the nature of raids. But, as we in England know, the best philosophers are not always professors. The fact is that the Americans are not a thoughtful people; they are too busy to stop and question their values. But they are developing an architecture which some think the finest in the world, and great architecture has before now been the beginning of greatness in other arts.

If we were sure that our weary Titan was handing over some of his duties and responsibilities to a people of this type—generous, kindly, just, and strenuous—we might think that world-power could not be in better hands. But is this fine old Puritan type likely to be permanent? The descendants of our colonists were as fine a race as any in the world; but the Civil War dealt them a heavy blow; racially, the nation has never recovered from it. Owing to the differential birth rate, America becomes less Anglo-Saxon every year, and its power of assimilating alien stocks must not be exaggerated. The Americans are realising, rather too late, the danger which besets them from the multitudes of Jews, Armenians, Neapolitans, and Russians whom they have allowed to flood their country. Immigration has not even greatly increased the population; it has substituted workers with a lower standard for the Americans who, in consequence of their presence, have not been born. A still more deadly blow to the Puritan tradition has been dealt by allowing many millions of Irish to settle in the country. These immigrants are more dangerous to the solidarity of the American type than the negroes, because the negroes cannot long tolerate the hard winters of the North and Middle West. Tuberculosis kills them off.

Democracy, as Santayana truly says, implies an optimistic assumption that at bottom all men's interests are compatible, and a public spirit such that no sectional interest shall rebel and try to maintain itself absolutely. It is the absence of this spirit in Europe which will probably bring our democracy to an end. Will it also wreck democracy in America, which now stands like a wall against sectional treasons and coddling socialism? There are few more important questions than this for the future of civilisation. European society will hardly break up while America remains sound, but it will not stand if America breaks up.

1924.

VIII

ROYALTY

THE FLAG AND THE THRONE

THIS is not a review of Sir Sidney Lee's *Life of Edward VII*, which I have not yet read. But the eager interest with which the publication of this book was awaited gives food for reflection. There is no doubt that the British people, in this democratic age, are far more interested in the Royal Family than our ancestors were in the time of "the Four Georges." It is also certain that many Americans, and a few Englishmen, cannot understand this interest.

Let us make a comparison, or contrast, with what happens in the United States. An American citizen, a prohibitionist on strike, fell on his face in the gutter. Rising to his feet, he wiped his hands on the nearest object resembling a towel, which happened to be the Stars and Stripes hanging out of a shop window. Another American citizen came by and knocked him down. He did this not because he cared for "Old Glory," but because he also was drunk and wanted to fight. He was arrested by a police-man and brought before a magistrate on a charge of assault and battery. While awaiting the proceedings, he bethought himself of pleading that he had acted hastily, because his patriotic feelings were excited by an outrage on the National Flag. The magistrate not only dismissed the case, but requested the honour of shaking hands with such a model citizen. The newspapers took the matter up, and thousands of pounds were subscribed to buy a suitable residence for the noble fellow.

Now if this had happened in England, say at Ascot, and the tipsy man had wiped his fingers on the coat of King Edward, there is not the slightest doubt what His Majesty would have said, but there the incident would probably have ended. If a bystander had knocked the man down, he would presumably have been fined about five shillings, and certainly nobody would have bought him a house.

Why do our cousins treat a piece of bunting as a religious emblem, and think it an antiquated prejudice to feel reverence for a human being who represents the nation? Homage to a flag or a mace seems to be a halfway house between loyalty to the person of the chief magistrate and no loyalty at all, which is the consistent attitude of the Socialists, who snort at the Union Jack.

Foreign observers, like President Lowell of Harvard, have noticed that very considerable powers still belong by law to the King of England; that in practice nearly all these powers are exercised by his servants; and that concurrently with this change, "the objections to the monarchy have almost entirely disappeared, and there is no republican sentiment left to-day either in Parliament or in the country." "It would very much surprise people," says Bagehot, "if they were told how many things the Queen could do without consulting Parliament. She could disband the Army and dismiss all the officers from the Commander-in-Chief downwards; she could dismiss all the sailors and sell off all our ships of war; she could make a peace by the sacrifice of Cornwall, and begin a war for the conquest of Brittany. She could make every citizen, male and female, a peer; she could make every parish a university; she could dismiss most of the civil servants, and pardon all offenders." The law of England, as Lowell says, is perfectly distinct from the conventions of the constitution; profound changes have not been enacted, they have just happened. Meanwhile, the President of the United States has retained, and actually exercises, much the same powers which were enjoyed by George III. at the time when the Americans broke off from the Empire.

The great popularity of the Royal Family began with Queen Victoria. The first two Georges were foreigners; "Farmer George" was certainly liked, but his attempts to govern by means of parliamentary influence—corruption would not be too strong a word—were unfortunate for the nation, and made him many enemies. His sons were not a credit to the family. Queen Victoria was idolised in the latter part of her reign; if she had died in middle life, her long retirement after her husband's death would have told against her memory. It must be admitted that her fame has suffered somewhat from recent revelations. Her interventions in foreign policy seem to have been influenced by narrow dynastic considerations; and she did her best to drag us into a war with Russia from which we had nothing to gain. Sir Sidney Lee's book, I am told, exposes the astonishing unwisdom of Prince Edward's education. The Prince Consort is revealed as a German pedant of the most extreme kind, forcing a bookish education on a boy who had no tastes or aptitude for study, and nervously keeping him away from any experience of life. I do not know whether Sir Sidney Lee has got hold of the delicious story of the proposed visit of the Prince of Italy in 1858, which was forbidden because the Queen feared that the coarse conversation of King Victor Emmanuel might "injure his innocence." Cavour in a letter to the Sardinian Minister in London, wrote: "Si on parle de ce voyage, vous pouvez rassurer La Cour sur le sort de cette qualité précieuse du Prince héréditaire. Si elle arrive avec lui à Turin, ce n'est pas ici qu'il la perdra." Cavour must have thoroughly enjoyed inditing this letter.

When I was in Germany two or three years before the war, I found a universal conviction that King Edward personally directed the foreign policy of England, and that his policy was to ally himself with France and "encircle" Germany. Sir Sidney Lee's second volume will doubtless throw new light on the King's Continental activities. We may be sure that he will be revealed as a clever diplomatist, but certainly not as an intriguer, nor as overstepping his constitutional position to carry out a policy of his own. Personal predilections no doubt counted for something. He liked the French, and, we are now assured, cordially disliked and distrusted Wilhelm II. The German ex-Emperor has steadily lost in the estimation of the world since his abdication. Almost everything that comes out about him lowers his reputation; and in particular, it is now absolutely certain that he was a false and treacherous friend to this country. King Edward seems to have been a shrewd judge of character; he saw through the Kaiser, as Lord Salisbury did; Rhodes and Chamberlain were perhaps taken in by him.

With the death of King Edward, the personal influence of the monarch on public policy came to an end, for a time. But the popularity of the Crown has never been greater than it is now, at least since the reign of Queen Elizabeth. There is always the possibility that a King of commanding character and outstanding ability may some day revive the dormant powers of the monarchy. But few would desire this, especially after what is now known of the personal rule of Wilhelm II. and Francis Joseph, and the deplorable incapacity of the unfortunate Nicholas of Russia. A genius on the throne may govern more efficiently and cheaply than any Parliament. There have been two or three great rulers who owed their position to the accident of birth. But such examples must be very rare exceptions; and the training of an heir apparent, with the temptations to which he is exposed, is not a good preparation for a dictator. If the hereditary principle is abandoned, and monarchy retained, the result is a struggle for power between ambitious men, generally soldiers, as happened in the Roman Empire. Prætorianism—government by military *pronunciamientos*—is a miserable form of government; it tears an empire to pieces, and exhausts the nation by civil wars. Dictatorships are best looked upon as emergency measures, an alternative preferable to anarchy. The American system of electing a chief magistrate and giving him considerable power for a few years, seems to be successful; but it has not yet been exposed to a severe strain. America has the immense advantages of being both half empty and invulnerable.

There is much to be said for our present system of making the King the head of the social organisation of the country, with only nominal political power. Our King receives much of the loyalty and devotion which Americans pay to their flag. The Throne is the least criticised and apparently the most stable of all our institutions; and if its occupant is just a good specimen of an English gentleman, that is what most of his subjects wish him to be. We have seen enough of clever sovereigns abroad; perhaps we have had enough of clever prime ministers at home.

1924.

IX

CAPITAL PUNISHMENT

"Should capital punishment be abolished?" is a favourite subject in school debating societies, and always produces an animated discussion. But the question has many sides, and deserves the close attention of grown men.

There have always been two views about punishment in general. Perhaps the most popular opinion now is that punishment should never be vindictive, but always reformatory or deterrent. Vengeance, it is said, belongs only to the Deity, or perhaps not even to the Deity, since hell is now very much out of favour. Society has the right to protect itself by making crime dangerous to the transgressor, and it has the duty to reform the criminal, if he can be reformed. On the other side, it is argued that it is immoral to punish a man for any other reason than because his actions deserve punishment; to chastise him in order to frighten others is unjust.

Reformatory punishment is not punishment at all.

It is merely a method of treatment which happens to be painful. We do not speak of a surgeon punishing his patient, though he may put him to great discomfort. The word punishment should in my opinion be confined to penalties which are in intention a retribution for anti-social conduct. If this motive is repudiated, deterrent legislation can hardly be called just to the individual who is sentenced. In point of fact, many offences are punished vindictively. A murderer is hanged on the principle of "a life for a life," and certain vices are treated with extreme severity, perhaps because we still half unconsciously think that they bring pollution upon the community —a very wide-spread motive of criminal legislation in primitive societies.

I can see nothing immoral or unreasonable in regarding the criminal law as the instrument of the outraged conscience of the nation. This was St. Paul's opinion. He speaks of the magistrate as "the minister of God, an avenger to execute wrath upon him that doeth evil." Of course, if we suppose that the Deity himself never feels wrath and never punishes retributively, the State cannot claim the right to do so either. In that case, in the strict sense, nobody ought to be "punished" at all. But though this view is held by many Christians, it is incompatible with Christianity.

Capital punishment obviously cannot be reformatory, but it is in the highest degree deterrent.   Many now think that the State has no right to take away a man's life.   Oddly enough, this view is usually held by revolutionaries, who manage to combine it with a readiness to massacre all who do not agree with them.   In several continental countries capital punishment has been abolished, and solitary confinement for life substituted for it.   Thus an extremely cruel penalty has been substituted for a merciful one.

I have often found a queer notion that the Bible sanctions, or rather prescribes, the death sentence for murder, but forbids it in all other cases. Apart from the absurdity of treating a verse in Genesis as a revelation for all time of the limits of criminal justice, it is notorious that the legislation of the Old Testament prescribes death for many other offences besides murder, including sabbath-breaking and adultery.   It is only lately that murder has been put in a class by itself.   A hundred years ago there was a long list of capital offences, and minor offenders were sentenced to death by the score every year, though only a small fraction of them were actually executed.   Public opinion would now disapprove of the death penalty except for wilful murder, and every execution, even for an atrocious murder, causes many searchings of heart.   What are the reasons for this comparatively recent scruple about taking life?

Executions are said to be cruel.   And so they are, but not quite in the way that the objectors usually mean it.   Hanging used to mean death by strangulation, a rather slow and agonising death, as is testified by the authors of *The Road to Endor*, the young officers who hanged themselves as part of their pretence to be mad and were cut down only just in time. Now the criminal has his neck broken, which might be done just as well without putting a rope around his neck.   He thus escapes physical suffering altogether. But the importance of this has surely been greatly exaggerated.   Granted that in old days the criminal had five or ten minutes of torture before death released him, most of us would be glad to know that our last illness will cause us only ten minutes of severe pain.

Nature's executions are on an average far more cruel than man's.   The cruelty of our present system is moral, not physical cruelty.   It consists partly in the wholly unnecessary degradation and humiliation of an English execution—contrast a modern hanging with Plato's account of the execution of Socrates in prison.   But much more, it consists in the long-drawn mental agony to which the criminal is subjected and in the horrible publicity of a murder trial.

An exciting murder trial gives the British public more pleasure than the gladiatorial combats and the tortures of the Christian martyrs gave to the Roman populace, and the pleasure is of the same kind. If this is not monstrous cruelty, I do not know what is. And it does not strike the victims equally. The more self-respect the criminal and his family have possessed, the more horrible is their suffering. The whole family shares in the humiliation; their name is henceforth a disgrace; it is a name (if an unusual one) which nobody would willingly be known by. Have we the right to treat any human being in this way?

Some murderers, no doubt, are cold-blooded and heartless villains; others have yielded to sudden temptation, or are persons who, without being legally mad, are of morbid and unbalanced temperament. We do not know, and we cannot judge, the amount of moral guilt which attaches to any murderer. Men are not responsible for inborn vicious and criminal propensities. They are a disease rather than a fault, and we must leave judgment to God, who knows all. We do not sum up a man by calling him a murderer. We cannot hang a man for murder without hanging by the same rope three or four other men who do not deserve to be put to death. Many who have suffered death on the scaffold have by no means been destitute of good qualities. Others have been certainly abnormal and not fully responsible for their actions.

I plead for a complete change in our attitude towards capital punishment. I would abolish hanging, and I would abolish the death penalty as a necessary result of a conviction for murder. I would also plead earnestly for a moral change in the public mind, a change which would make people heartily ashamed of the ghoulish satisfaction which they now find in enjoying the disgrace and humiliation of a fellow-citizen. The Psalmist says: "Mine eyes gush out with water, because men keep not Thy law." I am afraid the British public is very far removed from this state of mind.

And yet I do not at all agree with those who think that the State has no right to take life. We have to protect ourselves against the enemies of society; and if it is fairly certain that a criminal is irreclaimable, that he must be, as long as he lives, a pest and a danger to his fellow-citizens, it is right that he should be removed. Sometimes, even after a conviction for murder, it would be worth while to detain the criminal for a year or more, putting him under moral and religious discipline, supervised by experts in morbid psychology who would, in some cases, be able to certify that he was apparently cured and fit to be at large. But there are some habitual criminals, not

murderers, whom it would be much better to put
out of the way.   They are a burden on the community while they are in prison, and as soon as they
are released they return to their old courses.

Executions, when they are ordered, ought to be
carried out without exposing the criminal to any
unnecessary disgrace.   They would not be a punishment, any more than the killing of a mad dog is a
punishment, and it would be understood that they
do not involve any moral judgment upon his character as apart from his actions.   The criminal who is
condemned to die ought to be humanely extinguished
in a lethal chamber, with as little publicity as possible, and no infamy ought to attach to his family any
more than when a member of a family is certified a
lunatic.

The objection may be made that the death penalty
would not be sufficiently deterrent, if this change
were made.   I do not think that cruel punishments
have much effect in diminishing crime.   Their chief
effect is to make juries reluctant to convict.   Pas-
sionate appeals to the compassion of the jury have
procured the acquittal of several murderers, of whose
guilt there is not much doubt.   The infliction of
death should never follow automatically upon conviction; it should be decided by careful investigation
and observation of the character and tendencies of

the convict, the crucial question being whether he is curable or not.

The change which I advocate would, I believe, remove a reproach from our system of justice and a source of demoralisation from the public.

1922.

X

REVOLUTIONS

THE maintenance of law and order in a civilised country depends partly on the force kept in reserve by the Government, and available, if necessary, to supplement the police and the magistrates, partly on the good-will and loyalty of the population as a whole, and partly on mere inertia and tradition and the habit of obedience to the laws. Changes are always going on, necessitating political and social readjustments. A rapid increase in population, the transformation of an agricultural into an industrial community, the spread of education, the shifting of the centre of gravity from one class or one locality to another—these and other changes oblige a State to modify its institutions. Sometimes, as at present in most civilised countries, the change is in the direction of democracy; at other periods the evolution of States has favoured the centralising of power in a few hands. There is no uniform line of progress.

But, on the whole, life in a civilised country becomes more and more complex. Organised society makes greater demands upon its members; the burden of civilisation becomes heavier in each generation. For this reason civilisation is a fragile thing; history shows that after a time the intrinsic qualities of the population no longer enable them to shoulder the burden. The chief cause of this failure is that civilisation tends to sterilise the ablest part of a nation. In each generation it skims off the cream and leaves the milk thinner.

There is in every country a class which is constitutionally unfit for civilised life. Certain races, whose abnormal fecundity enables them to contaminate better stocks, seem to have this disability. As Professor McBride says: "The Iberian or Mediterranean race is now found relatively pure in the South and West of Ireland, in Portugal, in Southern Italy, and in Egypt. Everywhere it exhibits the same characteristics—a fiery temper quick to take offence and to revenge an insult real or fancied; an utter absence of scruple in the weapons chosen to attack an enemy, assassination being preferred to open combat; a tendency to form secret societies and conspiracies; an utter disregard of truth, and an incapacity for perseverance in work."

"The influx of such lower elements into civilised societies," says Mr. Lothrop Stoddard (a brilliant

American writer) "is an unmitigated disaster. It upsets living standards, socially sterilises the higher native stocks, and if interbreeding occurs, the racial foundations of civilisation are undermined, and the mongrelised population sinks to a lower plane."

The subman, thus generated, or thrown off by the higher races (a farmer is said to expect one "wreckling" in every brood of pigs), hates the civilisation which he cannot share. He is in instinctive and natural revolt against civilisation as such. Every society engenders within itself hordes of savages and barbarians, ripe for revolt and eager to destroy.

Anatole France has drawn a masterly picture of a revolution in *Les Dieux Ont Soif*. The hero, a typical revolutionary leader, when led to execution amid the curses of the populace, laments that he has been too merciful—he has allowed a few of the "aristocrats" to escape.

Jack Cade, in Shakespeare, is a perfect Bolshevist type. "All the realm shall be in common. There shall be no money; all shall eat and drink on my score; and I will apparel them all in one livery that they may agree like brothers." A "boorjooi" is brought before him—a clerk who confesses that he can read and write. "Hang him with his pen and inkhorn about his neck" is the order of this precursor of Trotsky. "Burn all the records of the realm," he cries. "My mouth shall be the Parliament of England."

It is no accident that Russia, largely inhabited by thinly veneered Tartars, an uncivilisable race, has been the scene of the supreme triumph of the sub-man. Bolshevism is no new thing there. The revolt of Pugachef, in the reign of Catharine II., lasted three years, and was marked by the same excesses. In the decade before the war Russia was ravaged by the "Hooligans," criminal terrorists who carried on a civil war against society. As a Russian writer said in 1913, "there are no moral laws for the Hooligan. He values nothing and recognizes nothing. In the bloody madness of his acts there is always something deeply blasphemous, disgusting, purely bestial."

This class is the raw material of revolutions. They are kept under in normal times by the organised forces of civilisation; but when the social structure is shaken by war or famine or serious disturbance, they seize their opportunity and gather together for a spring.

They usually find able leaders. These are drawn from various sources. Some of them are fairly normal individuals, who have met with ill-luck or injustice, and are eager to be revenged upon a society which has not taken them at their own valuation.

Others are men of superior talent, spoilt by some mental or moral twist, which has destroyed their prospects of success in life. Others are young and impatient intellectuals, who exclaim, like Omar Khayyam,

> Ah, Love, could you and I with him conspire
> To grasp this sorry scheme of things entire,
>   Would we not shatter it to bits, and then
> Remould it nearer to the heart's desire?

Of this last class Mr. Stoddard says:

"The misguided superior is probably the most pathetic figure in human history. Flattered by designing scoundrels, used to sanctify sinister schemes, and pushed forward as a figurehead during the early stages of revolutionary agitation, the triumph of the revolution brings him to a tragic end. The underman turns upon his former champion with a snarl and tramples him into the mud."

When the subman gets his innings, though he has a short life and a merry one, he may do irreparable damage, especially in a highly-organised state. Russia has been almost literally decapitated, by the extermination of all its intelligent citizens; the materials for recovery in that unhappy country no longer exist. And the ruin in a more advanced community would be even more complete.

It has often been observed that a revolution be-comes steadily more savage and anarchical till it ends. The delirious ravings of Babeuf, in 1796, throw into the shade the rhetoric of Robespierre. But even Babeuf has been surpassed by the utter-ances of more modern revolutionaries like Bakunin and Sorel. Two gems of eloquence from these gentry may be quoted. In his *Revolutionary Catechism* (1848) Bakunin writes: "If you kill an unjust judge, you may be understood to mean merely that you think judges ought to be just; but if you go out of your way to kill a just judge, it is clear that you ob-ject to judges altogether. If a son kills a bad father, the act, though meritorious in its way, does not take us much further. But if he kills a good father, it cuts at the roots of all that pestilent system of family affection and loving-kindness and gratitude on which the present system is largely based." More recently Sorel, the Syndicalist, writes: "To repay with black ingratitude the benevolence of those who would protect the worker, to meet with insults the speeches of those who advocate human brotherhood, to reply by blows to the advocates of those who would propagate social peace, is a very practical method of showing the bourgeois that they must mind their own business." Proudhon howls: "I shall arm my-self to the teeth against civilisation. God—that is folly and cowardice; God is tyranny and misery; God is evil. Give me Satan." These demoniacs, remember, have a world-wide reputation and thousands of admirers.

I am not an alarmist. Civilisation, with all the sciences, and especially biology, which has completely undermined the philosophy of the subman, on its side, will probably be too strong for these criminal lunatics. But it is true that civilisation is being poisoned by its own waste products, by the rotten human material that we protect and foster so carefully. A correct diagnosis of the disease is important.

The disease is not due to defective institutions. The revolution, as I have shown, aims at destroying all social order as such. It wishes to exterminate all culture ("Burn all the Raphaels," says one of its spokesmen) as culture. The degenerate would leave nothing to remind him of his degeneracy.

It is not a class revolt, except that the subman naturally sinks to the bottom. The subman is emphatically not the working man. These vermin are spawned by all classes. Chicherin, like Mirabeau, is an aristocrat; Lenin and Trotsky, like most of the French revolutionists, are bourgeois; several anarchists are morbid and perverted men of letters, like Rousseau.

There is only one remedy—that by which hydrophobia has been extirpated. Suppress the mad dogs before they begin to bite, for the disease is contagious.

1922.

XI

"ENGLAND"

THIS is the simple title of a book by "An Overseas Englishman." It is a very timely book. It was high time that this long-suffering and down-trodden nation, which the Scotsman Lord Rosebery was once kind enough to call the predominant partner in the United Kingdom, should make a protest and speak up for itself.

"There are still in England," says our author, "some millions of this reticent and retiring race, and these have had leisure of late to reflect that their Prime Minister was a Welshman; that the leader of the great English armies in the great world war was a Scotsman; the captain of their great Navy an Irishman; the leader of the House of Commons an Irish Canadian; the Foreign Minister a Scotsman; their late Chief Justice (now the ruler of India) a Jew. In the administration of the Empire which England founded and long ruled, scarce a third are now Englishmen!"

And yet it is England which invented parliamentary institutions, which gave its language and laws to the British Isles, and produced our immortal literature; it is England which taught honour and manliness, kindliness, fair play and toleration to a world which much needed and has as yet only half-learnt these English lessons.

We have acquiesced in the "unhistoric and pinchbeck title of British," as Mr. Thomas Hardy calls it, and our newspapers are beginning to use the deliberately insulting Americanism "Britisher," just out of good nature and a mistaken idea of modesty. It is time to cry a halt!

I take up my parable as a man who is proud to be a pure Englishman, with no admixture of Scottish, Irish, Welsh or other blood for at least three hundred years, before which date my family does not seem to have been recognised by the College of Heralds. Judging by my patronymic, I suppose my ancestor "came over" as a Scandinavian pirate, and was, I dare say, as great a ruffian as most of William the Conqueror's Normans; but history is silent. "In spite of all temptations to belong to other nations," I am glad to be an Englishman pure and simple.

I have just been reading a fine book, *Soliloquies in England*, by the philosopher George Santayana, a Spanish North American, who loves our country and its people with a delicate and discriminating affection which warms the heart and makes one long to thank him personally. The book is full of wit and wisdom, and is written in the most charming style. He finds in us "a spirit of free co-operation," and says:

"This slow co-operation of free men, this liberty in democracy, is wholly English in its personal bias, its reserve, its tenacity, its empiricism, its public spirit, and its assurance of its own rightness, and it deserves to be called English always, to whatever countries it may spread. The general instinct is to run and help, to assume direction, to pull through somehow by mutual adaptation and by seizing on the readiest practical measures and working compromises."

So the German Karl Peters, a blackguard but a very shrewd observer, answers the question, "From what special quality does the empire-building faculty of the English spring?" by saying, "The strong sense of individual self-reliance is the most salient factor. The system of organised liberty holds sway in every English settlement. The Englishman must be his own law giver; but he is also possessed of a strong sense of law and order and a strong sense of fair play. What is 'fair' is at the bottom of all his legislative enactments." Mr. Winston Churchill speaks of "that sense of detachment and impartiality, that power of comprehending the other man's point of view," which has always been the secret of our success in administrating alien countries and provinces. The claim is just.

The habit of blaming and criticising our own country is ingrained among Englishmen, and when it is practised by sincere patriots it does good. The British lion always rouses himself to fresh efforts by lashing himself with his tail. But undoubtedly it encourages our enemies to defame us, when they hear us accusing ourselves. And unfortunately it also encourages the noxious breed of domestic traitors, the friends of their country's enemies for the time being, who whenever England is in difficulties try to make out that their country is in the wrong. Whether we are contending against white, black or brown antagonists, these disinterested friends of the human race (except England) come forward with their advocacy of the other side. We differ, it would seem, from all other misguided persons by never being in the right, even by accident. But it will generally be found that the anti-English Englishman has alien blood in his veins.

We have never done ourselves more injustice than during the war. To read the reports, it might be supposed that all the best work was done by Australasian, Canadian, Scottish, and Irish regiments.

Every feat of arms performed by the gallant soldiers from the Dominions was duly chronicled; the exploits of the English troops, who were by far the largest contingent, were passed over. Our Allies were not the people to rectify this injustice; their were some shameful scenes in more than one Allied capital, when our splendid regiments were insulted by the populace.

But the facts are known to those who care to know them. Whether or not it is true,[1] as a prominent Canadian asserted, that our War Office deliberately suppressed accounts of English heroism and English successes, it is now certain that the English regiments were the backbone of the Western front, and especially the old county regiments, such as the Worcesters, the Shropshires, the Devons, and the Hampshires. Special praise was occasionally given to a nominally Irish regiment, of which 75 per cent. were Englishmen.

Lord Rawlinson was at length impelled to speak his mind. "I have often," he said, "had the choice as to the disposition of troops on the field of battle; but where there has been a point that it was really important to hold, when there has been a tactical area which we could not afford to lose, it has always been English troops that I have chosen. . . . Of

[1] The War Office tells me that it is not true.

the troops that I have had under my command, the Englishman has done best."

But does the British nation still possess the qualities which made us great? Are they perhaps the virtues of an aristocratic class which set the tone for the whole nation, but has now fallen from influence and power? Is not the governing Englishman, whom Rudyard Kipling describes so lovingly, just a glorified public schoolboy?

It is true that the working man seems disposed to surrender our imperial heritage without much thought, and that he feels strangely little indignation at the insolence and crimes of rebels against the central authority. But, as the "Overseas Englishman" points out, very few of the bad type of labour leaders are Englishmen; and it will take time for the newly enfranchised class to realise the value of the inheritance which has now passed into their keeping.

But there were no class differences in the conduct of the men at the front. I think and hope that our author is right when he says: "In moments of moral crisis the English aristocrat and the English ploughman act exactly the same, and the way they act is different from the way of the Latin or the Celt, the Teuton, and the Slav."

I have long felt great admiration for a passage in Matthew Arnold's *Friendship's Garland*, in which an

Englishman is represented as lamenting to a German professor that the English have lost their vigour and fibre, and are becoming a feeble and flabby race. The German replies, in effect: "You need not trouble yourself about that. You are wretchedly unprepared and disorganised; but the character of your people is just what it always was." This half-forgotten little book reads like a prophecy. Our physical deterioration is, I am afraid, a fact; but if we will take to heart the warnings of the eugenists, it is not too late to mend.

All this boasting, I shall be told, is in very bad taste and very un-English. So it is; but events have given to me, as to other Englishmen, much food for thought; "and while I was thus musing, the fire kindled, and at last I spake with my tongue."

1922.

XII

THE JEWS

MR. HILAIRE BELLOC's book on *The Jews* has been and will be widely discussed. He dedicates it to a Jewish lady, and writes with studied moderation, protesting that he is anything rather than an anti-Semite. And yet nearly every page reminds us that during the Dreyfus agitation Mr. Belloc was almost the only man in England who did not take the part of the unfortunate prisoner. Either he believed in the guilt of the Jewish captain, or he agreed with the schoolboy who translated the French proverb: "Le jeu ne vaut pas la chandelle," "The Jew is not worth the scandal." It will be odd if the Jews do not regard this book as an attack on their race.

The fact is that Mr. Belloc, as a Frenchman and a Roman Catholic, takes the Continental rather than the English view of what he calls the Jewish problem. We think that every country gets the Jews that it deserves; and that we, who treat our Jewish fellow-citizens with decency, have both deserved and got

171

the best Jews.   It is contrary to all our traditions to
do what Mr. Belloc wishes us to do—to refuse to
forget a man's racial origin while he lives among us as
a good Englishman.   Above all other nations, we
English accept a man for what he is worth, and do
not penalise him because he is an immigrant.   The
result, is, as I said, that the English are the only
really downtrodden race in Europe.   We have a
Welsh Prime Minister, two Scotch archbishops, and
any number of Jews, Scots, and Irish in prominent
places.   But by so doing we are better served, and
we have enriched our stock by blending it with
desirable foreigners of all sorts.

How many of our best families are descended from
French Huguenots, and how many other Frenchmen,
like Mr. Belloc himself, have been welcomed in
England, much to our advantage! Similarly, a
large number of our most distinguished men and
women are partly Jewish by descent.   Mr. Belloc
himself mentions the Arnold family (I believe
wrongly), Robert Browning, and General Booth of
the Salvation Army.   What possible good could
there be in telling such people that they are "aliens?"

It is a flaw in Mr. Belloc's book that he says nothing about the religious side of the question.   The
motive of the omission may be guessed at.   He objects to the Jews because their loyalty is divided—

they may, and often do, set their obligations to their own people above their allegiance to the country where they live. But the same is undeniably true of another class in Great Britain—Mr. Belloc's co-religionists. The Roman Catholics have in our history been far more troublesome citizens than the Jews.

He mentions the expulsion of the Jews from England by Edward I. as a surprising measure, but he does not tell us what the Jews themselves thought about it. They put it down to "the Papal merchants and the Pope's usurers, who have supplanted us." The Jews never plotted to assassinate the English Sovereign, as the Roman Catholics plotted to kill Queen Elizabeth; nor have the Jewish rabbis ever condoned murder, as the Irish priests are accused of doing to-day. It seems that the isolation of the Jews, which Mr. Belloc recommends, is part of the fixed policy of his Church. "The Catholic Church," he says, "is the conservator of an age-long European tradition, and that tradition will never compromise with the fiction that a Jew can be other than a Jew."

It is perhaps best not to say too much about the traditional method of treating Jews. I remember reading the précis of a trial before the Spanish Inquisition, describing the prolonged and hideous tortures inflicted on an unfortunate lady, who was accused of not eating pork, and of wearing clean linen on Saturday. The poor lady was a Spaniard; I do not think that the racial question has ever interested the Church. From its point of view a Jew can always cease to be a Jew by being baptised.

Are the Jews really so radically different from ourselves? I have known many and I cannot see it. They have, on the whole, a rather high level of intelligence, and, as Mr. Belloc says, more concentration than most English people. If the Jew wants to be a rich man, he is apt to be keener about his business than a Gentile; but if he has no ambition to make money, and chooses to be a philosopher, or a musician, he will often show a noble indifference to filthy lucre, like Spinoza. This Mr. Belloc admits. Even this concentration is by no means characteristic of all Jews. It is not their fault that they have been excluded from agriculture and similar pursuits. Few things in the Old Testament are more interesting than the evident determination of their lawgivers to keep the Israelites on the land, if possible. They were not to forget the time before they settled in Canaan, when they wandered with their flocks and herds. It was not by their own choice that they were impounded in Ghettos, or driven to money-lending.

There is a curious passage in Mr. Belloc's book in

which he complains of the sense of superiority which, he says, the Jews are unable to conceal. "On his side," he adds, "the Jew must recognise, however unpalatable to him the recognition may be, that those among whom he is living regard him as something much less than themselves." I venture to doubt whether any Englishman, meeting a Jew in society, ever dreams of asking himself whether his neighbour belongs to a superior or to an inferior race. The question would seem to most of us quite absurd. We judge people by their personal qualities, not by their nationality.

The most interesting part of this book discusses the connection of the Jews with Bolshevism. I confess that I have been sceptical about the accusation that "Bolshevism is a Jewish movement" on the ground that the Jew is the last person who would wish to see private property abolished. But Mr. Belloc shows that though the Jewish millionaires are very much in evidence, there are not many of them, and that the race as a whole is extremely poor. The Jew may or may not be as revengeful by nature as Shakespeare's Shylock, but even a nation schooled to sufferance must have harboured bitter feelings against the government of the Tsars, and against the Russian people, who unquestionably enjoyed the Jew-hunts which they called pogroms. There is, however, reason to suspect that the reports of these pogroms which appeared in western newspapers were sometimes exaggerated, and though the poor Jews in Russia are numerous, they do not seem at any time to have taken a very active part in a revolutionary outbreak.

Any international movement, whether capitalistic or communistic, is sure to utilise Jewish brains and Jewish cosmopolitanism, and it is no way surprising that the rascally Jew Braunstein, who disguises himself as Trotsky, should be one of the Red leaders. Nor is there anything unlikely in the story that Jews took an active part in the horrible murder of the Russian Royal Family.

But even if the Jews are more deeply concerned in Bolshevism than these admissions imply, I am disposed to trace their action in a rather different direction from Mr. Belloc. We must remember that the Russian Revolution was to a large extent made in Germany. The downfall of the Russian Government and the dissolution of the Russian Army and Empire was an object of the very greatest importance to the Germans, and their close business relations with Russia gave them an opportunity of carrying out their sinister purpose with skill and thoroughness. But for German gold and German treachery, it is very doubtful whether the Russian Communists

would ever have come into power. Is it not probable
that the German Government, in hatching this plot,
made great use of German and Russian Jews? It
seems to me likely, for the following reason: German
industrial capital is mainly Jewish; Russian industrial capital (what there was of it) was mainly
Russian. It seems quite possible that German-
Jewish commercial and industrial firms hoped by
destroying Russian industrialism to clear the way for
the future exploitation of the country by German-
Jewish capital. It is highly probable that when the
terrorists in Russia have fallen, the reconstruction
of the country will be largely financed by German
Jews.

I once heard a dignified clergyman say pompously;
"We owe the Jews more than we can ever repay."
To which I felt inclined to answer: "I hope, sir, that
in your case it is only a temporary embarrassment."
But seriously, we ought to be ashamed of anti-
Jewish prejudice. We do not follow Houston Chamberlain in his theory that Jesus Christ (like Agamem-
non, Dante, Shakespeare, and other great men) was
a German. We have been taught to believe that He
was a Jew. And in any case it seems inconsistent,
after annexing the sacred books of the Hebrews and
using them every day in our devotions, to cherish a
dislike against the race which produced them.

Above all, race-consciousness is a rather silly thing. The sensible man takes his neighbours as he finds them, and is not too ready to believe in dark conspiracies.

1922.

III
Social

THE BIRTH RATE

IT is a bad symptom that Lord Dawson's paper on Birth Control at the Birmingham Church Congress, wise and temperate and in perfect taste, should have been received in certain quarters with denunciation. The newspapers which have taken the lead in this agitation have probably mistaken the mind of their public; if not, they cannot be congratulated on their clientèle.

In dealing with a subject where so much ignorance and prejudice have been proved to exist, it is best to begin with a dispassionate and colourless statement of elementary facts.

The reproductive capacity of every species is far in excess of the possibility of survival. In some of the lower forms of life the fertility is prodigious. The star-fish has 200 million eggs. "If all the progeny of one oyster survived and multiplied, its great-great-grand-offspring would number 66 with 33 noughts after it, and the heap of shells would be eight times the size of our earth."

Fertility and care for offspring usually vary inversely. Sutherland says: "Of species that exhibit no sort of paternal care, the average of 49 gives 1,040,000 eggs to a female each year, while among those which make nests or any apology for nests the number is only about 10,000. Amongst those which have any protective tricks, such as carrying the eggs in pouches, or attached to the body, or in the mouth, the average number is under 1000, while among those which . . . bring the young into the world alive an average of 56 eggs is quite sufficient."

Man is no exception to this rule. Where the natural checks of famine, pestilence, inter-tribal slaughter, and disease operate without hindrance, the equilibrium of population is maintained by a very high birth rate. In the Middle Ages the births and deaths in the undrained towns were both round about 50 per thousand in each year.

There are cities in Asia where these conditions still survive. Almost everywhere the numbers press constantly upon the means of subsistence, and children can only survive where there is room for them. In many parts of the world, both in the civilised races of antiquity and among barbarous races in our own day, surplus children are got rid of by systematic infanticide.

If we look at old pedigrees, or at old tombstones covered with the names of one family, we shall see that a married pair in England, till the nineteenth century, might expect to lose more than half their children in their own lifetime. These children were of course not murdered, but nothing effective was done to keep them alive.

The population of a country is determined by economic laws, not by the will of individuals. Individuals may exercise choice, but numbers, like water, find their own level. Every unwanted baby, kept alive by humanitarian interference, drives another baby out of the world or prevents him from coming into it.

Depopulation is a somewhat rare phenomenon, and is generally caused by a change in the climate, exhaustion of the soil, or the diversion of trade routes. The depopulation of Mesopotamia followed necessarily on the destruction of the irrigation system by the Mongol hordes. The physiological infertility which is exterminating the physically splendid races in the South Sea Islands is another matter. It is a rare disease, and the causes of it have not been fully cleared up.

It is of course possible for a nation to increase its

numbers by expropriating another nation.   Merely to subjugate another nation is worse than useless, because the conquered people, being driven to a lower standard of living, will probably multiply faster than their conquerors.   It is no use even to massacre all the fighting men.   But if the women and children can be driven from their homes, and their lands seized by the invaders, then no doubt the conquerors may multiply up to the limits imposed by the size and fertility of the occupied territory.

This is the real meaning of "the right to expand," of which we have heard so much.   It is a pleasant prospect, if every nation with a high birth rate has a "right" to exterminate its neighbours.   Perhaps a quotation from Prince von Bülow's *Imperial Germany* will bring home to my readers what this claim means, and what calamities it has brought upon the world.   "The course of events has driven German policy out from the narrow confines of Europe into the wider world.   The nation, as it grew, burst the bounds of its old home, and its policy was dictated by its new needs.   The Empire could no longer support the immense mass of humanity within its boundaries.   Owing to the enormous increase of population German policy was confronted with a tremendous problem.   This had to be solved, if foreign countries were not to profit by the superfluity of German life which the mother country was unable to support." Mr. Harold Cox even says: "In the era upon which we have now entered the one fundamental cause of war is the overgrowth of the world's population."

I do not entirely agree with these two writers, because it is impossible for a country to have at any time a much larger population than it can support; but in the main they are right. The supposed duty of multiplication, and the alleged right to expand, are among the chief causes of modern war; and I repeat that if they justify war, it must be a war of extermination, since mere conquest does nothing to solve the problem.

The enormous increase in the population of Europe during the nineteenth century is a phenomenon quite unique in history. It was the result of the industrial revolution, combined with the opening out of new food-producing areas beyond the seas. The two new conditions reacted upon each other. Vast quantities of commodities could be produced cheaply, and they could be exchanged for food, while the improved methods of transport made the exchange possible and easy.

The process went on merrily at first because the new countries produced far more food than they needed for themselves. So there was a demand at home for more labour. The State, as shortsighted as governments usually are, applied an artificial stimulus to the birth rate by a Poor Law which encouraged irresponsible parentage, and permitted the Poor Law guardians to send wagon-loads of little children to work in the factories of the north. Till about the end of the last century every new pair of hands in England paid its way on the average, though the birth rate began to decline, in response to the falling death rate, after 1878.

But the new countries are getting filled up. The United States can feed itself, but not much more. Even the wheat-fields of Canada and the Argentine are not unlimited. And we in England have long since lost the privileged position in manufacture which we held for a considerable time after the war with Napoleon.

An abnormal era of expansion has reached its natural end. We cannot support more than our present population, and though there are still a few countries where a young Englishman of the right sort may emigrate with decidedly better prospects than he would have at home, there are no longer any wide empty tracts of good land waiting for occupation. Emigration, in a word, is a palliative only; and before long it will cease to be even a palliative.

Maps of the world are very delusive; they do not always mark the deserts, and there are many other unpleasant explanations of the empty spaces which look so alluring.

These, then, are the facts. The natural rate of human increase never has been and never can be attained. An equilibrium between births and deaths is the normal state of things: the nineteenth century was not normal, but unique. There are no more empty Americas and Australias, and, equally important, we have no longer any great surplus of manufactured goods, because the producers of those goods have begun to ask why they should not enjoy themselves. The *Expansion of England*, over which Sir John Seeley gloated so eloquently, was a grand thing while it lasted, except for the barbarians whose lands we took from them, but it has reached its natural and inevitable limit. We must cut our coat according to our cloth and adapt ourselves to changing circumstances.

Till the beginning of the war the birth rate and death rate in this country declined in parallel lines, the annual increase of population remaining very steady, at about one per cent. per annum. The utter absurdity of talking about "race suicide" is apparent to anyone who has the slightest knowledge of the subject. The decline in the birth rate was made necessary by the improvements in sanitation and medical science, which increased the average duration of life by about one third. The birth rate also declined by about one third, the maximum in the 'seventies being 36 per thousand, and the minimum before the war just under 24.

It is however highly probable that before long our present population may have to be reduced, for we cannot feed ourselves except by exporting articles which other nations can now make more cheaply than we can. Fortunately, we are not so far from an equilibrium as the figures of the Registrar General might lead us to suppose. The crude birth rate is about 13, which would give the average duration of life as 80 years! The actual expectation of life at birth for the two sexes together is about 55 years, which gives a death rate of 18 per thousand, calculated on the basis of a stationary population. The discrepancy is caused by the preponderance of young lives with a very low death rate; for instance, the death rate at 12 and 13, the healthiest years of life, is only two per thousand. As the age distribution of the population becomes more normal, as it will in consequence of the fall in the birth rate, the crude death rate will rise automatically to meet the real death rate, as has already happened in France, which is sometimes spoken of as an unhealthy country for this reason. The Frenchman really lives almost as long as the Englishman.

I know of no other subject on which ignorance is so gross and so unteachable, as this subject of vital statistics.

II

"CONSUMPTIONISM"

"CONSUMPTIONISM" is not a pretty word. It is defined by Mr. Samuel Strauss, in the *Atlantic Monthly*, as the science of compelling people to use more and more things. His contention is that this is not only a new science but a new necessity; that things are in the saddle and rule mankind, especially in America. It is, for most Americans, a matter for complacency and self-congratulation. The American artisan boasts that he has more comforts and conveniences than kings had two hundred years ago; he has his motor-car and his bath-room, his vacuum cleaners, cameras, 'bus lines, telephones, picture palaces, best-selling novels, and what-not. Production must go on at an ever increasing speed; otherwise there would be a decline in the volume of business, which is not to be thought of. But the chief problem is not how to produce enough; machinery has solved that difficulty; the problem is how to make men want and use more than enough—how to make them desire what at present they are content to do without. The machines demand a steady rise in the standard of living, and the science of "consumptionism" consists in raising the standard by persuading the consumer that he wants more and more every year.

This is probably the driving force in the Prohibition movement. Superficially it was a moral and religious agitation; melancholy pictures were drawn of young men going to the bad through drink, beating their wives and robbing their employers. But drunkenness was never a national vice in America, and after a time the tone of the agitators changed. Alcohol, they said, is a nuisance because it diminishes output. It is bad for the factory. There is no longer any pretence that the sole object of prohibition is to prevent drunkenness; it has swept the entire people into its net. And the real purpose of this tyrannical legislation is to increase the consumption of other commodities. Mr. Henry Ford, for example, sees that without prohibition he would not sell four million motor-cars a year. Drink gives a man a substitute for the satisfaction which the acquirement of luxuries brings; the more drink men have the less things they need, and the less money they have to buy them. This is contrary to the philosophy of consumptionism. Consequently, according to Mr. Strauss, the Eighteenth Amendment to the Constitution, enforcing prohibition, was placed on the statute book.

There are other important consequences of this new science, or necessity, or philosophy. The American newspapers, we are told, now exist not so much to direct men how to think, feel, and vote, as to teach them how to buy. They are coming to be, before all else, instruments for those desires and needs which men have most in common. For this reason, newspapers which formerly represented rather different points of view on politics or social questions are constantly amalgamating. Advertisers much prefer a few newspapers with large circulations, and they can offer better terms to such newspapers. The old system of numerous papers, each the organ of one distinct type of opinion, was good democracy, but bad business. The new journalism, with its "mammoth combines," is good business, but bad democracy.

I do not altogether agree with Mr. Strauss that Western civilisation is in the grip of a tyrannical machine which it can no longer control. We might infer from his view of the situation that the only remedy would be to abolish all machinery by law, like Samuel Butler's Erewhonians, or to smash the machines like the gangs of "Captain Swing" in the early days of the industrial revolution. I should rather say that the present orgy of "consumption-ism" will continue just as long as it seems to most people a desirable ideal. Ideals are the strongest things in the world, and in this case a change of ideals would operate decisively without any drastic State action. We have only to remember how the haymaking of the profiteer after the war was brought to a sudden end by a sort of consumers' strike. The consumers struck, no doubt, mainly because they had no more money; but they might have struck because they had no more taste for lavish and need-lees expenditure. The consumer has always the last word, because the longer his strike continues, the stronger his position becomes. And as soon as he asks, "Am I really getting my money's worth?" the advertiser and traveller will appeal to him in vain.

We are really brought back to two rival philoso-phies of life, which have divided mankind since men first began to think and to choose their way of living. We have to balance our account with our environ-ment, and the sum may be represented as a vulgar fraction, the numerator being what we have, and the denominator what we want. We may bring them together either by increasing our numerator, which is the wisdom of the West, or by diminishing our denominator, which is the wisdom of the East. Which is the right method of solving the problem?

The art of living is not best understood by highly industrialised communities, where men are too busy to think, and where the cult of efficiency makes them reluctant to waste time, as they put it, by considering whether their standards of value correspond with the nature of things and with their own best selves. But we ought not to evade these questions. For it is an unpleasant reflection that the same motives which make big business hostile to sensual gratifications must make it antagonistic to all the higher interests of life—to art, science, philosophy, and religion. For all these are in one way like drink—they "make men desire fewer things." A philosopher was once asked by a vulgar fellow whether his philosophy had ever brought him in any money. The answer, intended to be intelligible to the questioner, was: "It has saved me a great many expenses." Consumptionism plainly has no use for philosophy!

And what of Christianity? We can hardly doubt that when St. Paul says, "Having food and raiment, let us be therewith content," he is interpreting correctly what the Gospel has to teach us about the art of living well and wisely. It does not seem that the science of increasing men's wants is on the lines of the teaching of Christ.

This is not a question on which all Conservatives will be found on one side and all Socialists on the other. There are still many prosperous citizens who are open to the satire of the lines beginning:

Now Dives daily feasted and was gorgeously arrayed,
Not at all because he liked it, but because 'twas good for
    trade—

a fallacy which John Stuart Mill exposed once for all. And on the other side, Marx or Engels, I forget which, complained bitterly of "the accursed absence of wants" among the poor as the chief obstacle to his revolutionary propaganda. Only last week Mr. Wheatley declared that if the working man would demand more money and spend more on his comforts, there would be an end of unemployment. Mr. Wheatley is probably not so foolish as to believe this, but it suits him to make his clients believe it, and it is a common argument with Socialist agitators.

But it will not do. The demands of the "average sensual man," in Matthew Arnold's phrase, are in their nature insatiable, as Plato told us long before the Christian revelation. Wordsworth's line, "Getting and spending, we lay waste our powers," cuts at the root of the philosophy of consumptionism. We are not really wiser or better or happier by complicating our lives, by using mechanical inventions to turn luxuries into comforts, and comforts into necessaries.   The tyrant is not the machine, from which we may free ourselves when we will, but the insatiable cravings of the lower nature.   While we try to gratify every desire, we "never once possess our souls before we die."   The extreme wastefulness of modern civilisation ought to alarm us.   We are recklessly using up the natural resources of the planet, as well as defacing its beauty beyond repair. Civilisation is becoming more and more artificial, and therefore more and more precarious.   There is a way which seemeth right unto a man, but the end thereof are the ways of death.

The East, to sum up, has much to teach the West in these matters, and perhaps we may be willing to learn, now that the West is uneasily conscious that the civilisation of the East may menace our own, and perhaps outlast it.   The Indian and Chinese peasant, with his frugal wants, based on immemorial tradition, may have a greater survival value than the American artisan with his £1,000 a year, his Ford car, his bejewelled wife, and his daily visit to the "movies."

We must strike a balance between the two ideals, of course; we do not want to go back to Diogenes and his tub; but if "consumptionism" is the enemy of high thinking as well as of plain living, it is no ideal for us.

1924.

III

THE RIGHTS OF ANIMALS

FROM time to time in the course of history some great discovery or revelation is made which not only adds to the store of human knowledge, but carries with it new and important moral obligations. The Christian revelation abolished in principle all artificial barriers between man and man, teaching that all races are of the same blood, and that "in Christ" there is neither Jew nor Greek, neither civilised man nor barbarian, neither white man nor black. This discovery ought to have put an end to war and social injustice, as it has, after a shamefully long time, put an end to slavery. But the new knowledge has had to contend with racial habits tens of thousands of years old; and when the cake of custom is suddenly broken, as it was in the Great War, optimists find to their dismay that human nature has not changed at all.

The last century produced a discovery nearly as important for ethics as that of the unity of mankind.

Darwin and his fellow-workers proved that all life in the world springs from one root, and that the lower animals are literally our distant cousins. There is nothing to be ashamed of in the relationship. But we can hardly suppose that the other animals, if they are able to think, admit our superiority. If they were capable of formulating a religion, they might differ considerably as to the shape of the benefi- cent Creator, but they would nearly all agree that the Devil must be very like a big white man. For we have always treated our poor relations in fur and feathers as if they had no rights at all. We have not only enslaved them, and killed and eaten them, but we have made it one of our chief pleasures to take away their lives, and not infrequently we have tortured them.

Our ancestors sinned in ignorance; they were taught (as I deeply regret to say one great Christian Church still teaches) that the world, with all that it contains, was made for man, and that the lower orders of creation have no claims whatever upon us. But we have no longer the excuse of saying that we do not know; we do know that organic life on this planet is all woven of one stuff, and that if we are children of our Heavenly Father, it must be true, as Christ told us, that no sparrow falls to the ground without His care. The new knowledge has revolutionised our ideas of our relations to the other living creatures who share the world with us, and it is our duty to consider seriously what this knowledge should mean for us in matters of conduct.

There are some worthy people who think that we ought to give up eating flesh. But we must eat something; and vegetables are, I suppose, our cousins, too, if we go back far enough. Besides, the result of general vegetarianism would be that many species would cease to exist. Nobody is so much interested in the demand for pork as the pig. I think, therefore, that we must accept the universal law of nature, which, as has been said, consists in the conjugation of the verb "to eat," in the active and passive.

The question of field-sports is much more difficult. The hunting instinct is as deeply rooted in mankind as the fighting instinct. It is so strong that one cannot think the worse of a man for being a sportsman. And yet I am strongly convinced that to make a pleasure of killing harmless beasts and birds is a barbarous thing, now that we know what science has taught us about our kinship with them. I believe that the time will come when the sportsman, instead of swaggering about railway-stations as he does now, will be fain to hide his tools, as the golfer who should have been at the front tried to smuggle away his clubs during the war.

My readers will not all agree with me here. But
there is another violation of the rights of animals
which ought to find no defenders. Deliberate
cruelty to our defenceless and beautiful little cousins
is surely one of the meanest and most detestable
vices of which a human being can be guilty. In this
country direct cruelty to animals is severely punished; but what is the difference between tearing off a
bird's wings yourself, and paying someone else to do
it for you? Women have no excuse for not knowing
how their egret plumes are procured. The hideous
story is matter of common knowledge. It is a disgrace to the country of Charles Darwin that such
trophies should be exhibited and admired. The
wearers should be made to feel that they are repulsive
objects, and not beautiful, as they suppose; and no
time should be lost in making the trade illegal.

Nor is hatred of cruelty the only reason for supporting this kind of legislation. It is reasonable to
infer that God made the world beautiful because
beauty is one of His own attributes, and is holy in His
sight. If this is so, it is a sin to deface the beauties
of nature, and to make the world hideous in our haste
to heap up money for ourselves. The insatiable
greed of man has invaded the sanctuaries of unspoilt
nature. It has scoured the woods and the moun-
tains and the prairies and the lonely islets where the

sea-birds make their habitations. Many beautiful species will be gone for ever in a few years unless the strong arm of the law puts a stop to the massacre.

It is for this country to take the lead in suppressing these outrages, which are a disgrace to civilisation, an offence against God, and a crime against posterity. Other nations, especially those in which the official teachers of religion and morals are the slaves of tradition, learning nothing and forgetting nothing, are sadly behindhand in this matter. With our wide Empire, we can do more than any other nation to protect animal life; and we may be quite sure of this —that if our legislators will have the courage to deal firmly with this evil, disregarding the protests of a small number of interested persons, they will be considered by future ages to have taken a step forward in civilisation, and to have thereby brought honour to their country.

1920.

IV

UTOPIAS

THE Utopian is a poet who has gone astray, forgetful of Milton's not very poetical warning, that "to sequester out of the world into Atlantic and Utopian politics, which can never be drawn into use, will not mend our condition." Perhaps some Utopians do not hope to mend our condition. Like W. H. Hudson in his delicately beautiful *Crystal Age*, they dream of a world in which they would like to live, and in which the fairy gift of imagination may help them and their readers to live for a time. Other Utopias are satires on existing conditions; they show the changes which might result if human nature were changed; but their authors may have but little hope of changing human nature.

Generally, however, Utopias are thrown either into the past or the future. Pictures of a golden past age are rather out of fashion. We are only slowly emerging from a century of apocalyptic hopes. Some of us, it is true, think of the happy days before the war, and wonder that we did not know when we were well off, but we are still too near the reign of Edward VII. to idealise it, and our children deride us if we weep for the spacious days of Queen Victoria. The young people say with Ovid:

Prisca iuvent alios; ego me nunc denique natum
Gratulor; haec aetas moribus apta meis.

And yet Utopias are really the creation of the race-memory, which gives voice to deeper instincts than what we are in the habit of calling the lessons of history. It is an erroneous notion that we know a great deal about the past and nothing about the future. The things that we know about the past may be divided into those which probably never happened and those which do not much matter. As Samuel Butler says, historians have the power, which is not claimed by the Deity, of altering the past; and this is perhaps the reason why they are allowed to exist. Historians, when they pretend to describe the past, are helping to make or mar the future. Utopias, on the other hand, are a revolt against modern trammels. Things are in the saddle and rule mankind. The horse wishes to fling up his heels now and then.

The making of Utopias is a masculine foible. I cannot recall any Utopia written by a woman; though most of them contain laws which women would resist either by the ancient method of a strike, as described by Aristophanes in the *Lysistrata*, or by the modern method of bombs.   Most Utopias have been written by Englishmen or Frenchmen.

At the bottom of most Utopias lies a consciousness of the deep unnaturalness of our civilisation.   As Taine says: "Twenty centuries of precepts hang over our heads."   Modern life is too complicated; we have too much of everything, including clothes.   It becomes more and more difficult to satisfy a continually growing mass of fictitious wants.   So the Utopians are usually primitivists.   They glorify the noble savage, who runs wild in woods.

Other evils which are attacked by Utopians are inequality, social injustice, poverty, overstrain and anxiety, and ugliness.   Most of them depict a race of beautiful human animals.   This we might have, if we were willing to pay the price, which is selective breeding.   But it is chiefly in quite modern Utopias that science is brought in.

In More's Utopia, private property is abolished, and gold is worthless.   The priests are few, and good; there are no lawyers.   At the time, the book was regarded as a satire rather than a scheme of possible reforms.   Utopians may be divided into the Utopians of innocence, or rather ignorance, like the Socialists, who take themselves very seriously as practical men, and the Utopians of experience, whose schemes are not much more than a plaything. More belonged to the second class. He knew that "it is not possible for all things to be well unless all men were good, which I think will not be yet for these many years." His reforms are such as "I may rather wish than hope after." But he is serious about land tenure and higher wages, and in advocating variety of employment, "streets twenty feet broad," and a garden to each house.

Bacon and Campanella, both authors of Utopias, were contemporaries. But the Calabrian monk spent twenty-seven years in prison and died obscure. Bacon is very modern, in two ways. He believed his reforms to be possible, and he believed in science. The salvation of society, he held, would come through "the knowledge of causes," "of the true nature of things." Like More, he is in favour of religious toleration. In Campanella the man of science and the Church disciplinarian meet. All is to be ordered by a kind of monastic rule. Communism is to be established, as in the monasteries, the only institutions in which Communism has yet been found possible. A universal four hours' working day is enforced. The best workers are to be honoured, and commerce is to be despised. He hoped that public spirit would make men work, but heavy penalties are proposed

against shirkers. This scheme recalls on one side
the Republic of Plato, who, as has often been said,
sketched out a polity which could only be realised
under something like a Catholic theocracy, and on
the other side the most extravagant proposals of the
so-called Labour party to reduce labour to a minimum.

Modern Utopias are much less playful, being, in
fact, programmes of social reform. They claim to
be judged by different standards from the earlier
books. To say: "You have forgotten human nature" is a valid criticism of Bellamy, William Morris,
Howells, Renouvier, Edward Carpenter, and Mr.
Wells (if they deserve it); it does not hit Sir Thomas
More, nor, among the moderns, Hudson and Samuel
Butler, of whom the former is a prose-poet, the latter
a satirist.

Utopias have for the present become Democratic
and Republican—a passing fashion, probably. The
Frenchman Cabet was a Communist, but he objected
to Babeuf's advocacy of violence to bring it about.
He belonged to the small and laudable class of experi-
mental Utopians. He went to America, and founded
an "Icaria" there, which dragged on for a good many
years as a squalid village. Cabet died, with all his
illusions gone, in 1856. All other attempts to found
ideal commonwealths have ended in dismal failure.

It was fortunate for the reputation of my favourite philosopher Plotinus, that the Emperor Gallienus refused him permission to found a "Platonopolis" in Campania, on a deserted and probably malarious site.

The French have rivalled the English in the wealth of their Utopian output. To those already mentioned must be added the names of Delacroix, Leconte de Lisle, Quinet, and Faguet. An ingenious prophecy of the state of Europe in 1997 was written by Daniel Halévy. The rural parts are depopulated —"albumen" has been manufactured and socialised, thereby solving the bread problem—all the people are in the towns—they have nothing to do except to go to shows and theatres, and to get drunk. A prohibitionist minority protests in vain—a new plague destroys half the population—an invasion by the Mohammedans of Asia and Africa is threatened—a good minority takes the reins, but are murdered by Russian Anarchists. The chief value of his book is his recognition of the dangers of idleness, and of the moral and social degeneration which would follow if a great nation became a "Land of the Do-as-you-Likes."

All serious Utopians are generated by undue disparagement and hatred of the present. It has become a habit of ardent reformers to represent this as

the worst of all possible civilisations, and to idealise
the past and the future by way of accentuating the
sins of the present.   We notice this tendency especially in armchair Socialists like Mr. Tawney.   We
can hardly do our generation a worse service than
by stirring up bitter and causeless discontent with
present conditions, under which the masses are better
off than they have ever been before.   We have made
a great mess of our opportunities, no doubt; so did
our ancestors, and so will our descendants.   We can
choose between a perfect commonwealth in the clouds
and an imperfect but tolerable one—a poor thing
but our own—on earth.

1924.

V

HAPPY PEOPLE

THE wise man who wrote the so-called Proverbs of Solomon says: "The heart knoweth its own bitterness, and a stranger doth not intermeddle with its joy." We really know very little about the people whom we meet. We see their faces, which are not much more than masks, but we cannot read their hearts. Robert Browning thanks God that the meanest of his creatures has two soul-sides, one to face the world with, one to show a woman when he loves her. It is only in the intimacy of family life, or in that rare thing, a perfect friendship, that the veil is partially drawn aside. And even then we do not lay bare our hearts entirely.

Who are really the happiest people? It is odd that we have no answer ready; for with most of us happiness is "our being's end and aim." We are sometimes in doubt whether our own balance is on the right side or the wrong. Looking back, I think I can separate the years when I was happy and those when I was unhappy. But perhaps at the time I should have judged differently. We are never either so happy or so miserable as we suppose ourselves to be.

The successful man generally tells us that he was happiest while he was still struggling for his success, or sometimes before he discovered that an ambitious career was open to him. As a rule, the game of life is worth playing, but the struggle is the prize.

It is generally supposed that the young are happier than the old. This seems to me very doubtful. Young people are often very unhappy, torn by conflicting elements in their characters, which, after a time, come to some kind of a mutual understanding. Robert Browning boldly claims that old age is "the best of life," and some old people agree with him.

The married are supposed to be happier than the single. They are certainly less prone to commit suicide; but suicide is not a very good test, and it has been pointed out that married people with no children are not much less suicidally inclined than bachelors and spinsters. Still, as a rule, marriage is probably the happiest state. It all depends on whether the pair are well matched, and very bad choices are, I think, the exception.

On the whole, the happiest people seem to be

those who have no particular cause for being happy except the fact that they are so—a good reason, no doubt. And yet I should not choose a naturally contented temperament as my first request from a fairy godmother. It would be unfortunate if I said, "I wish to be the happiest man in England," and promptly found myself locked up in an asylum, a cheerful lunatic who believed himself to be the Emperor of China. For all we know to the contrary, the happiest man in England may be a madman, and none of us would wish to change places with him. And even if the always cheerful person is perfectly sane, he is without the "splendid spur" which most men need if they are to do much with their lives. George Borrow, the author of *Lavengro*, thus addresses those who suffer from depression: "How dost thou know that this dark principle is not thy best friend? It may be the mother of wisdom and great works; it is the dread of the horror of the night which makes the pilgrim hasten on his way. When thou feelest it nigh, let thy safety word be Onward! If thou tarry, thou art overwhelmed. Courage! Build great works: 'tis urging thee—it is ever nearest the favourites of God—the fool knows little of it. Thou would'st be joyous, would'st thou? Then be a fool. What great work was ever the result of joy, the puny one? Who have been the wise ones, the mighty ones, the conquering ones of the earth? The joyous? I believe it not."

This is rhetorical. But I have noticed with surprise how often the biographies of great men reveal that they were subject to frequent and severe fits of depression, which the world knew nothing of. Perhaps it is only shallow natures who never feel the tragedy of existence. I can sympathise with the man who wrote: "Send me hence ten thousand miles, from a face which always smiles."

And yet those who might take comfort from Borrow's praise of melancholy have to remember that the Sermon on the Mount goes far towards ranking worry as one of the deadly sins. Spinoza agrees: Sadness (*tristitia*) is never justifiable, he says. The medieval monks, who must have known the moral dangers of boredom, placed among the Seven Deadly Sins one which they called Acedia. They describe it as a compound of dejection, sloth, and irritability, which makes a man feel that no good is worth doing. We have forgotten the word, and when we are attacked by the thing we blame our nerves or our livers. But perhaps the monks were right.

Religion is a great source of happiness, because it gives us the right standard of values, and enables us to regard our troubles as "a light affliction which is but for a moment." But the religious temperament is susceptible to more grievous fits of misery than any other.

We hear sometimes of the gaiety which prevails in a monastery or nunnery. I confess that this vapid spiritual hilarity rather irritates me. Running away from life ought not to make people happy. Unworldliness based on knowledge of the world is the finest thing on earth; but unworldliness based on ignorance of the world is less admirable.

Very different is the happiness enjoyed by such a saint as the Hindu mystic and Christian missionary, Sadhu Sundar Singh, whose life has just been written by Canon Streeter. It is one of the most fascinating books that I have read for a long time. The Sadhu has undergone every kind of persecution, including two days at the bottom of a well in Tibet, where he found himself among the decaying corpses of former victims. He lives the life of St. Francis of Assisi, and is as happy as that most Christlike of saints. An English parlourmaid announced him to her mistress as follows: "There's someone come to see you, ma'am. I can't make nothing of his name, but he looks as if he might be Jesus Christ." I urge my readers to read *The Sadhu*. It will make them feel better—or worse, which is much the same thing in this connection.

To descend from these heights. The busy are

happier than the idle, and the man who has found his work much happier than the man who has not found it.   Recognition by others is essential to all but the strongest and proudest virtue.   I think I should put it third among the gifts which I should ask from the fairy godmother above mentioned.   I should wish first for wisdom, like King Solomon; and by wisdom I mean a just estimate of the relative values of things. My second wish would be for domestic happiness, and my third for the approval of my fellows.

Napoleon is said to have recommended "a hard heart and a good digestion" as the chief conditions of happiness.   I have nothing to say against the second; but a life without affection and sympathy could give only a very negative kind of happiness.

Can we say that some periods of history were happier than others?   Nobody can doubt that we have fallen upon evil times; and it seems to be true that we take public affairs much more tragically than they did in the eighteenth century.   Dr. Johnson lived through the American war, the greatest misfortune that has ever happened to the British Empire.   But this is how he delivers himself about public calamities.   *Boswell:* "If I were in Parliament, I should be vexed if things went wrong."   *Johnson:* "That's cant, sir.   Public affairs vex no man." *Boswell:* "Have they not vexed yourself a little, sir?

Have you not been vexed by all the turbulence of this reign?" *Johnson:* "Sir, I have never slept an hour less, nor eat an ounce less meat."

We are not so philosophical. There must be many thousands of Englishmen who, like myself, were awake all night after the first ominous bulletin about Jutland, which seemed to hint at a great naval disaster. But all through the war, when things were looking bad, I tried to remember another scene from English history. We are told that in the days of the Commonwealth Bulstrode Whitelocke, Ambassador to The Hague, was tossing about through the night in anxiety about the condition of his country. An old servant, lying in the same room, addressed him: "Sir, may I ask you a question?" "Certainly," replied the Ambassador. "Sir, did God govern the world well before you came into it?" "Undoubtedly." "And will He rule the world well when you have gone out of it?" "Undoubtedly." "Then, sir, can you not trust Him to rule the world well while you are in it?" The tired Ambassador turned on his side and fell asleep.

1921.

VI

SPOON FEEDING

AT the season when the British *paterfamilias* is sending his children on their Christmas visit to the dentist it must occur to him to wonder why the noble savage never has any trouble with his teeth. It is said that they are kept healthy by the hard work they have to do in tearing tough meat without the help of knife and fork. These implements, and the art of cookery, are reducing man to a toothless animal, and are, perhaps, responsible for such evils as appendicitis and cancer, from which savages hardly suffer at all.

This is only a sample of what civilisation is doing to us, and civilisation, for the majority in every nation, is not yet a hundred years old. Until quite lately the housewife used to bake her own bread, make her own jam, and offer her friends home-brewed wine. Now she can do none of these things. The labourer, before the industrial revolution, was a

handy man, almost self-sufficing. Now he understands only one thing—perhaps how to punch out
biscuits from a slab of pulp without making the circles
intersect. Mr. Austin Freeman, whose observations
of savage peoples have made him keenly alive to the
evils of machinery, describes how his caravan was
overtaken by a storm in Central Africa. The na-
tives set to work in the forest, and in a few hours a
row of serviceable waterproof huts had been con-
structed. The despised savage would no more ask
the Government to spend a thousand pounds in
building a house for him than he would ask it to
comb his hair.

Every year we invent machines to do something
new for us. Handwriting used to be an art, and a
pretty one. Now an increasing number of people
rely entirely on the typewriter, and advertisers as-
sure us that "you cannot afford to do your writing
in the old way." When the typewriter has been introduced into schools we may have a generation who
cannot write at all.

Walking and riding, two delightful and health-
giving exercises, are becoming extinct. Two hundred years ago the roads were full of riders, and of
pedestrians who thought nothing of thirty miles a
day. The joys of a long country walk, either solitary
or with a friend, are unknown to the younger genera-

tion, although there is no more delightful way of
spending a spring or summer day.

The changes that have come over reading are less
obvious, but equally great. An ancient manuscript
fills us with wonder that men ever had eyesight and
patience enough for such reading. It must have
been a slow process—not altogether a disadvantage
when the book is a good one. Medieval manuscripts and early printed books are sometimes clear,
but often so minute as to try the strongest modern
eyes. And spectacles, probably poor ones at first,
are said to have been first discovered about 1300
A.D. No wonder, we think, that the Greeks disliked old age, when they had neither spectacles nor
false teeth. But they got on without them fairly
well, though they were a very long-lived race.
Sophocles wrote his last play, without spectacles,
when he was ninety.

The Germans, too, until very recently, made reading a painful exercise. They still like large and
closely printed pages, but when to this was added the
black-letter type, peculiarly trying to the eyes, and
the contorted German sentence, sprawling over half
a page, with the verbs, or parts of them, in a bunch
at the end, we cannot say that the path of learning
was made easy for the most diligent and plodding of
nations. Even in English, if we compare the prose

of the Sixteenth and Seventeenth Centuries with that which is written to-day, we shall find that the earlier prose demands real mental exercise on the part of the reader. Modern prose, even when written quickly for ephemeral purposes, may not be beautiful or dignified, but is generally clear. There is no difficulty in understanding what any sentence means, and writers are careful not to jolt the minds of their readers by anything obscure or ambiguous. Our books are now printed in good plain type.

Reading in these circumstances is purely receptive; it is not work at all. For most people it is an agreeable way of killing time, and obviating the painful necessity of thinking, when we have nothing else to do. Our journeyman fiction is evidently a means of getting away from real life, a mild anodyne, or a stimulus to day-dreaming. Newspaper-reading seems to be very largely the result of interest in vicarious athletics and in betting, topics which make no demand on the intellect whatever. There is also a wide desire for general information, but it is only the results, not the method by which they are arrived at, which interest the public. The newspapers are full of snippets, often very well written and illustrated, which give their readers the latest science in tabloid form. The pictures are all photographs;

here, again, we are watching the death of a fine art, that of drawing and engraving.

Education, except where the pupils are encouraged to make things with their own hands, is mainly spoon-feeding. Fifty years ago the editions of the classics were so bad that the student had to puzzle out difficulties for himself. Now he sits luxuriously before a crib, two commentaries, and a book of lecture-notes which have been slowly dictated in class. He need not use his brains at all. The battle between Greeks and Trojans in education has raged for many years; but the truth is that the conscientious tutor and the conscientious editor between them have killed the valuable part of a classical training.

The same process of making things easy is discernible even in games. Half a century ago the cricket coaches at Eton and Harrow used to bowl to the elevens down a slope, to teach them how to stop the famous Lord's shooters. Now if a ball shoots at Lord's, which it hardly ever does, it always gets a wicket, and the aggrieved batsman complains of the ground-man.   The modern mountaineer leaves it to others to "climb the steep ascent of heaven in peril, toil, and pain"; he prefers a more comfortable way of getting to the top—he "follows by the train."

Everywhere we find the same demand to make life easy, safe, and fool-proof.   The fine trees in our public parks are periodically mangled and reduced to the condition of clothes-props by our urban and county councils, because boughs have been known to be blown down in a high wind, or even, in the case of elm-trees, to fall suddenly, and once in two hundred years some fool might be standing under the tree at the moment. Every workman must be insured against every variety of accident, even when it is caused by his own negligence. If a traveller slips on a piece of orange-peel, which he ought to have seen, in a railway station, or allows his coat to be stolen under his eyes in a carriage, he brings an action against the railway company, and wins it. We now demand to be personally conducted through life, all risks to be taken by someone else. After a century or two of this régime we shall all be as helpless as Lord Avebury's ants, who starved almost to death in sight of food because they were used to having it put into their mouths by their slaves.

All this may be right, or it may only be inevitable. But do not let us deceive ourselves. Nature will make us pay for it. Nature takes away any faculty that is not used. She is taking away our natural defences, and has probably added nothing, since the beginning of the historical period, to our mental powers. The power of grappling with difficulties, and finding our way out of labyrinths, will soon be

lost if we no longer need it. And after any derange-
ment of our social order we might come to need it
very badly. Besides, can we look with satisfaction
at the completed product of civilisation, a creature
unable to masticate, to write, or to walk, a mere
parasite on the machines that enable him to live?
Many would prefer to be savages if they could have
the magnificent physique of the Zulus or some South
Sea Islanders.

There is a general slackness and dislike of unnecessary exertion among our younger people. It affects
their religion, which they like to have given them,
like everything else, in tabloid form, and without
any irksome demands upon their energies. This is
certainly not the way of the Cross, and it compares
badly with Michael Angelo's words: "Nothing makes
the soul so pure, so religious, as the endeavour to
create something perfect; for God is perfection, and
whoever strives for perfection strives for something
that is godlike"; or with Newton's "Genius is
patience."

But I refrain; for I hear my young friends saying
to me: "My venerable sir, when I am your age I shall
talk just like that, and I suppose I shall find some-
body to print it."

1924.

VII

MEDICAL SUPERSTITIONS

THOSE whose memories carry them back fifty years or more must have some queer recollections of the notions about health and disease which were prevalent in the Middle Victorian period. At that date it was still common to meet a man wearing a great coat in summer, with a woollen wrapper wound about his throat, and a respirator to prevent any pure air from entering his mouth. "Poor fellow! He is consumptive," was the explanation. We were probably told that he belonged to a consumptive family, and that one after another of his brothers and sisters had fallen victims to this hereditary disease. One or two doctors had already suggested that consumption might be infectious, but they were not listened to. If a medical officer had recommended burning down the family abode—a thing which was actually done the other day—after a third case of tuberculosis in the house—he would have been laughed at. Consumption, especially of the "galloping" variety, was a family curse, and primitive eugenics was as emphatic against marrying into a "consumptive family" as against marrying a first cousin—an indiscretion which was supposed to involve the direst consequences.

Fevers were catalogued as "high" or "low." Those who worked their minds too hard were liable to "brain fever," which no doubt was "high." Even the medical profession did not distinguish between typhus and typhoid, though the two diseases are totally different.

All children were taught that if they cut themselves between the first finger and thumb they would probably die of lockjaw. It had not occurred to anyone that that is the place where one is likely to cut oneself with a dirty garden knife.

"Internal inflammation" covered a multitude of sins, including all cases of appendicitis. But we were warned that if we swallowed a fruit-stone it might find its way into the "cherrystone pouch," and then we should die.

Drunkards, we were informed, died not only of delirium tremens, but of "spontaneous combustion," an awful fate described by Dickens.

The dangers of childbirth were enormously exaggerated, and every well-brought-up young woman prepared for the worst before the birth of her first baby. The revisers of the Prayer Book are now at last considering whether the words "great pain and peril" do not overstate the facts.

In treatment, the general principle was that whatever the patient wished to do was probably the worst thing for him.   His inclinations were not his own, but were suggested by "the disease," and so his attendants would stand no nonsense.   If he was hot and feverish, more blankets were added; if he gasped for breath, the window was shut more tightly; if he refused to eat, he was stuffed with food; and if he went to sleep he was awakened with a shake.

George Eliot describes two rival practitioners, one of whom believed in "the lowering treatment," while the other liked too see his patients "well padded against the shafts of disease."   Most people, like Shakespeare's Julius Cæsar, liked to have about them men that were fat, though in the eighteenth century Charlotte Elizabeth, mother of the Regent of France, records a tragic case of a lady who was found dead in bed, "suffocated by her own fat, which had melted from the great heat."   My nurses had a poor opinion of my chances of longevity, because, like Cassius, I had a lean and hungry look, and thought too much.

A strange superstition, which still survived in my childhood, was that the night air is poisonous.   This idea was almost universal in the eighteenth century, and still flourishes on the Continent, even where there are no malarial mosquitoes to give it some justification. A writer on "The Diseases of the Eighteenth Century," says that the medical treatises of the age are full of sad examples of young ladies of beauty, fortune, and great merit who on the eve of being married went to bed perfectly well and "woke up stone dead" of an inflammatory sore throat caught by a night air. I fancy that among the poor this superstition is far from extinct even now.

The notion that washing is dangerous had been discredited long before my memory begins, but a hundred and fifty years ago the maxim for ablutions seems to have been, "Hands often, feet seldom, head never!" Fifty years ago there was a rage for cold baths, even in winter, and on a January morning the family would ask each other at breakfast, "Did you find ice in your bath?" which would be satisfactorily answered by all except little Tommy, who made the shocking confession, "I don't know."

The cold bath was, indeed, the only form of asceticism practised by English Protestants. It has not survived the diffusion of bathrooms with "hot and cold." I have been told that in parts of England the miners think it dangerous to apply water to the spine, and never wash the middle line of the backs. If this is a libel, I duly apologise for it.

Children were encouraged to gorge themselves with food, especially with butcher's meat, which would make them as strong as the oxen whose flesh they devoured. I have seen schoolboys of that generation blue in the face at the end of a meal, in the presence of their approving parents. Adults ate more than they do now—far more meat, at any rate; but the gormandising age was rather earlier.

There is not the least doubt that most well-to-do people under the Four Georges shortened their lives considerably by eating and drinking too much. It is no accident that the few persons who lived to old age at that time are generally recorded to have been abstemious. It is pathetic to compare the portraits of Charles James Fox and his contemporaries as Eton boys with the gross old gentlemen "forty years on," who bore the same names.

Gout ravaged the aristocracy a hundred years ago. The victims were rather proud of it, so long as it was understood that it was "rich man's gout," which comes from drinking too much, and not "poor man's gout," which comes from eating too little. It was believed that this affliction was inherited, though it was observed that "talent and gout sometimes skip a generation." The fathers consumed too many sweet grapes, and the children's teeth were set on edge.

The practice of bleeding, still commemorated in the name of "The Lancet," had, of course, gone out before my childhood. The writer already quoted says: "Louis XIV. was bled generously (the adjective is his doctor's!) nine times in the scarlet fever. Bleeding killed the Duchesse de Tremouille in 1709, and her husband, who was bled to death to console him for her loss." When the mob attacked the Duke of Bedford's house in 1763, the doctors remedied the outrage by bleeding the Duchess next morning. When George Selwyn, at Lord Coventry's, fell against a marble table and cut his head open, a surgeon rushed upon him and bled him at once, though, to be sure, Nature was already doing it herself.

What has become of the early Victorian fainting-fit? Did our grandmothers really faint, or was it only a well-worked means of attraction for the other sex? The fainting-fit, or feinting-fit, seems to have succeeded "the spleen" and "the vapours," which can hardly have been very engaging. But fits of screaming seem to have attracted not only the attention but the compassion of our gallant ancestors, who regarded woman as a cross between an angel and an idiot, and petted her when she gave way to the weaknesses which were supposed to belong to her sex.

The advance in medical science and in popular

knowledge of hygiene in the last half century, has
been amazing.   There are still, however, many persons who do not scruple to dine out, or pay a visit,
while suffering from streaming colds, which are quite
as infectious as, and may be more serious than,
mumps or chicken-pox.

Will our grandchildren look back upon our ideas
about health as we look upon those of the early Victorians? I think not.   Perhaps the present fad for
removing superfluous organs may go out of fashion;
but modern hygiene is based on solid knowledge.
There are just 189 recognised ways of dying; a doctor
who lets a patient die in any other way has to explain
himself to the Registrar-General.

I do not know when the last verdict "Died by
act of God" was returned.   A judge defined this as
"a death for which no *rational* cause could be found."
I observe that in the latest Blue Book in my possession (1920), five of our 189 enemies—typhus,
yellow fever, cholera, rabies, and glanders—failed to
score.

1923.

VIII

PSYCHOTHERAPY

(I)

THE name Coué, which till lately would have auto-suggested a tale of adventure in the Australian bush, has now become famous in connection with the newest school of psychotherapy. M. Coué himself has been in London, and Society has fallen flat before him. The Australian bush-cry, Frenchified, still resounds in West-End drawing-rooms. His disciple, M. Charles Baudouin, has published a theoretical exposition of his method, the English translation of which has gone through several editions in a few months.

He and M. Coué have given the public exactly what the public wants to believe. The civilised world is being devastated by an orgy of irrationalism. The intellect is useless—how pleasant to know this, when it is so much trouble to cultivate it! The will is worse than useless; for the more men will to cure a bad habit, the more often they fall into it. That is just what we have always found; only stupid moralists have told us, "If at first you don't succeed, try, try, try again." And now we discover, with surprise and delight, that our guardian angel is the imagination, which surges up out of the deep pools of the subconscious, a mysterious but potent repository of all forgotten experiences and mental automatisms.

We are to train the subconscious, to coax it out of its hiding-places, to humbug it with soft words often repeated, until it flows over into our conscious life, submerging the stupid intellect and the interfering will; and then we shall become happy and good and perfectly healthy.

We are to make a habit of "relaxation." Sit in your most comfortable armchair, stretch out your arms and legs in the easiest posture, be very careful to think of nothing and wish for nothing, and wait for the subconscious to manifest itself.

As a student of the mystics, I have met with this sort of thing before. Complete detachment from all thought-images, quiescence of the will, passivity of all the faculties, have been recommended by all the mystics, from Plotinus to George Fox. But they have not prayed to their subconscious selves. They have called the exercise the practice of the presence of God; and they have not taken it in their most comfortable armchair—far from it.

M. Coué is wisely not content with the practice of passive contemplation. He recommends morning and evening prayer. Bury your face in the bedclothes, and repeat ten or twenty times, "with religious earnestness," the words: "Every day, in all respects, I am becoming better and better."

It is recommended to emphasise the words "in all respects," for they may effect the cure of maladies which have escaped the patient's notice. Well, the Christian also knows the benefit of morning and evening prayers; but he does not say them under the bedclothes, and instead of the formula: "Every day, in all respects, I am becoming better and better," he prefers: "God be merciful to me a sinner."

This epidemic of irrationalism has given us pragmatism in philosophy, magic and superstition in religion, antinomianism in morals, post-impressionism in art, and Bolshevism in politics. At least, they all come from the father of lies, so I suppose they are closely related to each other, and I think I can see some relation between them. They all begin by saying: "The true is what I choose to believe, and if I choose persistently enough I can make it so."

There is too much money in this kind of business; it is wise to be very sceptical. "Have faith in the remedy and it will cure you"; they all say it.

M. Baudouin is quite explicit. "Every new method for the treatment of chronic tuberculosis, provided that it is harmless, will give satisfactory
results."

What is the truth about these alleged cures? The
accepted medical opinion is that functional diseases,
particularly of the nervous system, can be benefited
by suggestion, but that organic disease cannot. I
once sat on a committee for investigating the subject,
and I asked the medical members whether there was
a hard and fast line between functional and organic
disease, and in particular whether it was impossible
that microbic diseases—a very large class—might be
benefited by "bucking up" the patient. The doctors admitted that the line was hard to draw.

M. Baudouin wishes us to believe that there is
no difference between organic and functional diseases, and that both alike are being cured by M.
Coué. He has no doubt that tumors may be cured
by suggestion, and entirely confirms the old folk-
belief that warts may be spirited away. One of
the medical witnesses at our committee described a
cure of locomotor ataxia by suggestion, adding that
of course the case had been wrongly diagnosed. It
is clear that much more investigation is required.

Unfortunately, it is peculiarly difficult to get at
the truth. On our committee, we found the priestly

curers rather shifty; and some organisations for faith-cure are prosperous businesses, to which an unsolicited advertisement from an expert committee would be invaluable. It is easy to see that M. Coué's patients, who have been lying to themselves every morning and evening "with religious earnestness" would be most untrustworthy witnesses as to the results of the treatment.

But some useful discoveries have been made. The use of hypnosis, which was formerly considered indispensable, has now been almost abandoned; and the newest school consider auto-suggestion much more efficacious than suggestion by others. M. Baudouin divides auto-suggestion into spontaneous and reflective, and gives both a place.

He is doubtless right in saying that we do ourselves much mischief by unregulated auto-suggestion; and thinks that prophecies by mediums, or by students of heredity, may sometimes bring about their own fulfilment to the great detriment of the subjects. Psychical epidemics, whether religious or patriotic or political, are best explained as the effect of mere imitation, an unconscious counterfeit. "In everything there is an element of suggestion."

He gives a strange example of the effects of obsession on an unborn child. Its mother was startled to notice that a visitor had a nail like a bird's claw.

Her child was born with the same finger deformed in the same way.

Long ago I heard a similar story. A young clergyman was driving a dogcart with his wife when they witnessed a sad accident—a child was knocked down by a wagon, and a wheel went over its face, obliterating the eyes. The clergyman drove off to the nearest village to fetch a doctor, while the wife, who was with child, held the head of the dying child on her lap. Her own child was born dead, with a deep mark across the face, obliterating the eyes.

A doctor to whom I repeated this story said that it is quite impossible; but evidently the time is come for re-examining such evidence without prejudice.

It is not surprising that M. Baudouin believes that we are unhappy because we cry, and happy because we laugh. He seriously recommends a man who suffers from mental depression to pull up the corners of his mouth.

M. Coué's advice to doctors will make him popular with dispensing chemists. Whenever a patient consults a doctor, the latter should always order some drug, even if drugs are not really indicated. What the patient wants is a bottle of medicine. The doctor, therefore, should always prescribe some medicine for his patient, and he should write his own prescriptions.

Well, for my own part, I will have nothing to do with this world of make-believe. It is an abomination to me. I believe that my reason was given to me that I may know things as they are, and my will that I may bring my refractory disposition into harmony with the laws of my Creator. I will neither twist up the corners of my mouth when I am in the dumps, nor tell myself that in all respects I am getting better and younger and handsomer every day. If I can help it, I will play no tricks with my soul, in the faith that though bluff may sometimes pay very well in this world, it will cut a very poor figure in the next.

IX

PSYCHOTHERAPY

(II)

I have read newspaper comments on my last week's article and have received several private letters. These latter testify that M. Coué is a man of the highest character and of transparent honesty, and that he is not using his reputation, as he might do without reproach, to make a fortune for himself. It is therefore right to dissociate him entirely from certain other healers, of whom it would be impossible to say the same. I understand that M. Coué does not even claim to be a healer; "*je ne suis pas un guérisseur,*" he has said. His claim is that his method liberates the *vis medicatrix naturæ*, which is inhibited in most persons by their want of faith, and by the depression caused by unfavourable medical verdicts.

The question what diseases can be benefited by suggestion, or by auto-suggestion, can only be decided by collecting and investigating a very large number of cases. Considering the vast amount of evidence that is available, it seems strange that so much uncertainty still exists. There are, however, several reasons which make the inquiries exceptionally difficult.

The first requirement is obviously a competent medical diagnosis. But doctors are fallible, like the rest of us; and those patients who are afterwards "cured" by suggestion may often be hypochondriacs who have simulated the symptoms of the disease which they describe to their physician. When we remember that many women have frightened themselves into simulating pregnancy, and have deceived even their doctors and nurses, it is hard to set any limit to the difficulties which hysteria may add to diagnosis.

Next, faith-healing is very much entangled with sacerdotal magic; and as no suggestion is more potent than that which is reinforced by religion, some of the most striking cures which have been reported are connected with alleged miraculous powers. But religious miracle-workers are not always very scrupulous, and they are very liable to be deceived, from lack of medical knowledge. A notorious imposter lived in clover at Lourdes for several years as a prize exhibit, and was only exposed when he took to committing other frauds.

Above all, the patient's own evidence is often

worthless. There is no absurdity which a patient under hypnosis cannot be induced to believe, as I know from what an Army doctor has told me. He persuaded perfectly normal soldiers that they had flown out of the window. We have to remember that as a hysterical patient simulates disease, so the subject of faith-cure frequently simulates recovery. He thinks himself cured; perhaps he feels no more pain; perhaps he is able to bend a stiff joint, and so on; but all the time an organic disease may be running a normal course, and the end may come as inevitably as if no treatment by suggestion had been tried.

I have heard of a case of internal cancer, at Albany, U. S. A., when the patient, after a course of Christian Science, declared herself cured, and went again into society. About six months afterwards she dropped dead, and the autopsy revealed the frightful ravages of the disease. I do not dispute that she got her money's worth out of the healers, for she was spared months of agony, but cure there was none.

Mr. Charles Sampson, who criticises me, speaks with authority, and has had great experience. But he seems to some extent to have misunderstood me. He contradicts my statement that hypnosis is being abandoned by practitioners of psycho-therapy. I should not have made this statement without first-hand evidence. M. Coué and M. Baudouin do not seem to use hypnosis, and more than one doctor who treats patients by suggestion has told me that he began with hypnotism but has discontinued it, because he finds that a quiet talk with the patient, without hypnosis, is equally efficacious.

Again, Mr. Sampson says: "Drug habits, alcoholism, insomnia, vice, all the functional neuroses, bad habits, the ghastly torments of pain in malignant disease, operations where anæsthetics could never with safety be administered—all these things can be overcome by medical hypnosis in the proper hands." I have no doubt that they can; I never denied it.

The most interesting witness before our committee was the Rev. Samuel McComb, D.D., of the Emmanuel Movement in America, who uses suggestion in connection with definite religious teaching. He has been specially successful in curing alcoholism, but other bad habits, and various neuroses, have also been treated by him with very good results. He always works with a doctor when he can, though he has taken a few cases which the doctors have given up. In answer to a question he replied: "Such evidence as I can find has failed to convince me that a truly organic disease can be cured by mental influence alone."

Social 241

That is the point. Most of these suggestion-systems claim to cure cases in which any doctor would say that there has been actual lesion of the nerve centres or destruction of some organ or tissue. Examples brought before our committee included cancer, cirrhosis of the liver, hip disease, pneumonia, toxæmia, erysipelas, dysentery, conjunctivitis, epilepsy, blindness, deafness, disseminated sclerosis, tetanus. In most of these cases there was no medical evidence.

M. Coué himself claims to have restored the sight of an eye which had been blind for twenty years, and explains that the idea that the eye was blind had "atrophied" the sense of perception. I am not a doctor, but would any medical man think it possible that an organ which had been functionally "atrophied" for twenty years could be restored to its normal condition by an exercise of the imagination?

One of the ablest doctors on the committee believed that "if by suggestion we can allay the unrest of a disturbing consciousness, we may permit the unconscious or subconscious functions a freer play." And that "if by suggestion we concentrate the mind upon a much-desired end—a healing result—we may at the same time more powerfully direct subconscious effort in co-operation." But he was quite convinced that we can expect no results when there has been actual organic injury.

To the outsider it seems that it ought to be possible to put the whole business of faith-healing on a scientific basis. The unexplored borderlands of science are the favourite breeding-grounds of superstition and quackery of all kinds. Materialistic science and unscientific religion left a wide gap which has been filled by a luxuriant growth of strange beliefs and cults. Let the physicians of the soul and the physicians of the body try to come nearer to each other, with the help of a sound psychology to mediate between them. Both sides would gain greatly by a better understanding, and the patients would gain most of all.

The study of suggestion is still, I think, in an early stage; otherwise there would not be so much difference of opinion on matters which an impartial examination of the evidence would soon clear up. When once the limits of psycho-therapeutics have been ascertained it ought to be possible to apply this treatment to appropriate cases without any hocus-pocus or self-deception. Then the quacks will find their occupation gone.

1922.

X

EUGENICS

FOR many old-fashioned people the science of Eugenics is summed up in the question whether first cousins ought to be allowed to marry. Unfortunately, this is one of the questions which have not been definitely cleared up. The answer would probably be that in a thoroughly healthy family there is no objection; but that there is a fairly long list of defects which tend to be hereditary, and that a double dose of any of these is undesirable.

Two persons who are inclined to go mad or to be epileptic had better not marry at all, and certainly should not marry each other. Tennyson, no doubt, said it was a good thing that Carlyle and Jane Welsh married each other, for otherwise there would have been four unhappy people instead of two; but that is not a convincing argument, though it has been used to justify the union of two deaf-mutes.

The eugenic objection to cousinly marriages, which is scientifically doubtful, is generally accepted because tradition has made it respectable; but the science of Eugenics as a whole is decidedly unpopular.

It is a new science, and a new science usually passes through three stages. At first the world says that it is nonsense; next, that it is contrary to Christianity; and, finally, that everybody knew it before.

The students of Eugenics are still exposed to ridicule and religious prejudice. They have been pilloried in fiction as wishing to interfere with the right of every man and woman to please themselves in the choice of mates. We have been invited to picture a state of society in which everybody is officially classified like the recruits in a conscript army, and compelled to marry according to schedule. Moralists have suspected them of wishing to introduce the methods of a stud-farm. Socialists are indignant at the suggestion that the pig sometimes makes the sty, and not the sty the pig, and that even when all property has been satisfactorily "transferred" ("Steal? A fico for the phrase! 'Convey' the wise it call," says Pistol, in Shakespeare), it may still be a problem how to gather grapes of thorns and figs of thistles.

Behind all these prejudices lies the revolt against natural law, which is one of the strongest tendencies of our time. Political economy, which tried to turn a dry light on the laws of supply and demand, has been discarded as "inhuman"; the investigation of the historical evidence for certain religious dogmas has been dismissed as "intellectualism" or "rationalism"; and the notion that the progress of humanity depends not on emotion and sentiment, but on the knowledge of nature's laws and obedience to them is extremely unwelcome. Dame Nature smiles and says nothing; "I am not fond of talking," Plotinus made her say; but presently she shows her refractory children the way to her capacious scrap-heap.

The author of the name Eugenics was Sir Francis Galton, one of the best and wisest men whom I have known personally. The Eugenics Education Society, which exists to investigate the forces under social control which tend towards the improvement or deterioration of the human stock, was founded before his death, and has done much good work in a quiet way, with very little popular support. It is quite sound, from the Christian point of view, on the question of marriage; it has no political bias; it does not consist of cranks; and it has only twice actively supported legislation, the two occasions being the Act for the care and segregation of the feeble-minded, and the campaign against contagious disease.

Its members believe that though the science of Eugenics is still in its infancy, it will sooner or later be of immense importance for the welfare of the human race.   The work of original research is, of course, being done by specialists, some of whom prefer to remain outside the society.

The specialists have already established some important discoveries.   The inheritance of liability to many diseases and defects, such as insanity, feeble-mindedness, epilepsy, deaf-mutism, cataract, hæmophilia—this is far from being a complete list— has been proved; and in certain maladies the curious law has been ascertained that the inheritance comes through females who are themselves immune. In the terminology of Mendel, these diseases are recessive in the female sex and dominant in the male. The abnormal fertility of the feeble-minded, which leads to the multiplication of the worst social types, is a sinister fact which quite justifies legislative precautions.   The descendants of one mental and moral imbecile have often supplied scores of inmates to prisons, workhouses, and penitentiaries.   The inheritance of unusual ability is equally well established, though the laws which determine it seem to act irregularly.   The record of such families as the Darwins, Coleridges, Wordsworths, Pollocks is enough to silence scepticism.   Some kinds of talent are more strongly inherited than others.   The names of Kennedy, Butler, Sidgwick, and one or two more, come up again and again in the lists of those who have won distinction in the classics at the universities.

The school of biometricians have also calculated the relative importance of nature and nurture in determining character, and have arrived by mathematical methods at the conclusion that nature is at least five times more important than nurture in deciding the qualities of any individual. This knowledge is only a fragment of what may be known hereafter; but it is enough to prevent many disastrous marriages, and to prove to politicians (if they cared to listen) that to tax and bully out of existence those families which have distinguished themselves in the past is to inflict an injury on the future which, from its nature, is irreparable.

But prudent eugenists are in no hurry to advocate legislation. The International Congress of Eugenics which is to meet shortly in New York will not concern itself with any special agitation. It is a common experience in many branches of science that the laws of nature are found to be more complex and difficult to calculate than was at first supposed. The pedigrees which are selected to exhibit the transmission of this or that quality or defect are no doubt quite accurate; but if we study the history of families whom we know, and in whom some of these abnormalities have shown themselves, we do not find that the rules work out so neatly. And nothing short of overwhelming probability will be accepted as a basis of legislation.

Besides, before we think of scientific stirpiculture, we must make up our minds what we wish to breed for. A whole crowd of questions comes up at once. Do we want the citizens of our model State to be well-developed all round, or to be specialised for the work which they have to do? Are we to have human mastiffs for policemen and human greyhounds for postmen? Are our professors and statesmen to be men with gigantic heads and feeble limbs, like the "Grand Lunar" in Mr. Wells's novel? Or should we aim at a society of moderately efficient Greek gods? Is the man of the future to be very muscular or very beautiful? Are these qualities worth aiming at for their own sakes, even if for practical purposes they are useless? These may be problems for the remote future.

At present nobody wants to go even as far as the King of Prussia, who married his regiment of very tall guardsmen to women also selected for their size, without consulting the wishes of any of the parties; but it is worth while for everyone to study his family history for the last three or four generations. Sometimes we shall find a speaking likeness of ourselves in a great-grandfather or great-uncle.

We shall often discover certain aptitudes and defects which seem to be persistent in our stock, and which we may expect to find in our children. For instance, some families are precocious, others develop late. Some are restless and ambitious, others are happiest with a small and safe fixed income. And if we have any influence over our children when they come to marriageable age, a knowledge of eugenics will sometimes enable us to prevent a son or daughter from marrying into a biologically bad family.

A good natural endowment, physical, mental, and moral, is more important, at any rate in these days, than an old coat-of-arms, or even than a fortune. An heiress is often the last survivor of a poor and dwindling stock. Galton was of the opinion that many able families have been extinguished by the "taint of heiress blood." And if we think of sending our children to seek their fortunes in a foreign country, eugenics will have something to teach us. It is not wise to send a blue-eyed and yellow-haired "Nordic" to a warm country where Northerners have never been able to live. Nor is it wise to encourage marriages between very different types, such as English and Japanese.

It ought to be a commonplace that if, from motives of humanity, we no longer allow natural selection to operate, we must put some kind of rational selection in its place. Otherwise, the gains of natural selection will gradually be lost and we shall go downhill.

1921.

XI

DIVORCE

THE newspapers are again full of the thorny subject of divorce. I do not envy those who think that there is a clear case either for or against the proposed changes. It is, in my opinion, the most difficult of all the problems which are now before the nation.

Lord Buckmaster thinks that the issue is merely between common sense and humanity on the one side, and ecclesiastical prejudice and tradition on the other. I was discussing the matter the other day with one of Lord Buckmaster's colleagues on the Bench, and found that he was entirely opposed to the new facilities for divorce, on grounds quite unconnected with the doctrine of the Church of England or of any other church. He thought that Lord Buckmaster's experience of a court which dissolves marriages in less time than it takes to solemnise them had not taught him much.

It is notorious that in a large percentage of divorce cases there has been flagrant collusion. A man finds that his wife has ceased to care for him, and has been unfaithful to him. Yielding perhaps to her importunities, and in accordance with the perverted code of honour which seems to prevail in such cases, he resolves to sacrifice his own reputation rather than hers. And so he takes a woman with him to an hotel at Brighton. Nothing wrong takes place between them, but a chambermaid is given a pound note to remember that she found them in the same room. In this way the trick is done. The guilty woman is legally the innocent party; the innocent husband is the guilty party. This frequency of collusion makes it almost impossible for the Church to draw a distinction in its treatment of divorced persons who have subsequently remarried. In many cases the "innocent party" is anything but innocent; and how can the ecclesiastical authorities go behind the decision of the law court?

The permission given by the law for the guilty pair to marry each other has caused the break-up of very many happy homes. It seems that in the majority of cases the husband and wife have lived amicably together for some years, and children have been born. Then the wife conceives an unlawful passion for another man, and writes coolly to her husband in this style: "Dear Edwin, I have gone away with Captain Corker. Divorce me. Yours, Angelina." So the marriage is dissolved, and in a short time the woman and her paramour become "the Corkers," people to be called upon and asked to dinner. Whatever other concessions are made, marriages of this kind ought to be absolutely forbidden.

The source of the mischief is the perverse and immoral morality which is now preached as well as practised, especially by our very modern novelists, who have much to answer for in corrupting the moral sense of the nation. The new theory of marriage seems to be something of this kind. The marriage vow is a declaration of ardent sexual emotion; and if at any time this feeling comes to be excited by another person, the continuance of married life becomes an outrage upon the higher feelings, and the gratification of what used to be called lust becomes a blissful self-expression of the personality.

The truth, of course, is that the marriage vow is not a declaration at all, but a promise of life-long love and fidelity. It is the most sacred and solemn obligation into which a man and woman ever enter, an obligation enforced by every consideration of honour, decency, justice and religion. To say that our affections are not under the control of our wills is to bestialize human nature and to strike at the root of the validity of all contracts.

We seldom realise how completely the freedom of social intercourse between men and women depends on the general acceptance of the sanctity of marriage. Things are very different in countries where virtue is supposed to depend on the absence of opportunity, and the woman is the chief sufferer. The pleasantest side of our civilisation—the ease with which innocent friendships are made between men and women—stands or falls with that Christian sex-morality which is now being openly flouted.

And yet I see that those who favour an extension of the grounds of divorce have much to say for themselves. I am not much impressed by Lord Buckmaster's hard cases. "Hard cases make bad law" is a maxim accepted by all lawyers. But the fewer the hard cases the better the law, and it seems to me that it might be safer, in the interests of morality, to grant divorce for crime, contagious diseases, incurable drunkenness, and brutal cruelty than for adultery.

There are some ecclesiastics who wish, on grounds of authority, to make marriage absolutely indissoluble. This view was put forward by a prominent English Bishop while giving evidence before the Royal Commission on Divorce. One of the Commissioners, a Scotch judge, said: "I observe, my lord, that you approve of the doctrine of the Roman

Catholic Church that marriage is indissoluble. May I ask whether you also approve of the *subterfuges* to which that Church notoriously has recourse when it wishes to evade the rigour of the law?" The question was very much to the point.

Besides this, can anyone say that the condition of married life was satisfactory in countries where no divorce was allowed? It was in those countries that the *ménage à trois*—the husband, the wife, and the wife's *amant*, became almost an institution. Church legislation has not, in fact, been consistently on the side of severity. The Eastern Orthodox Church has never been very strict, but few would wish Western Christendom to imitate the great moral laxity which prevails in the east of Europe.

The authority of Christ is decisive for Christians. But it is uncertain whether He meant to allow divorce for adultery; the text in the Gospels is disputed. Many scholars think that the exception represents the mind of the Church at a later date, and not the words of Christ. If He did admit the exception, He almost certainly meant to sanction re-marriage; divorce without the right to remarry was, I believe, unthought of at that time.

But the real difficulty in appealing to the Gospels is a different one. Our Lord, while on earth, was

not in a position to *repeal* either the Law of Moses
or the laws of the Roman Empire, nor did He ever
think of doing so. He was not *legislating* even for
the Church, since there was no Church to legislate
for; none of His disciples had any suspicion that
"the Church" was anything more than a brief stop-
gap till the Messianic Kingdom of God should come.

No; He merely declared that many things which
the law cannot prevent are forbidden by God, and
must not be done. The question how far a nominally Christian but really half-Pagan State ought to
imitate Moses in making allowance for "the hardness of men's hearts" never came within His purview. He did say that the marriage vow is absolutely sacred for all who take Him for their Master;
and this is really all that we can get from the much-
discussed utterances of Christ about marriage.

The Church is, I think, probably mistaken in ruling out such offences as I have mentioned as possible
grounds for civil divorce. But I feel much more
strongly that our chief need is the creation of a sound
public opinion, condemning adultery in all circumstances as a shameful thing, and sweeping aside
such apologies for lust as our novelists are now giving us. Permanent social ostracism and ecclesiastical excommunication could do much. But when
public opinion can be trusted to take the right side,

I should like to see adultery made a criminal offence, as it was by the Mosaic Law and in many other ancient codes. Or perhaps the right of private vengeance might be conceded.

An English girl, surprised at the extreme freedom allowed to unmarried girls in America, said to an American friend: "But is there not some danger that one of your friends might—well, forget himself?" "He might forget himself," she said, "but you bet he won't forget that I have a brother, and that my brother has a gun!" This, however, is a somewhat barbarous way of deterring offenders.

I am in hopes that a wholesome reaction in these matters may be near, and I am sure we ought all to work for it. There is nothing that poisons the life of a country more surely than anything which threatens the security, the confidence. and the purity of home life.

1923.

XII

BETTING

THIS, like Capital Punishment, is a favourite subject for school debating societies, and perhaps there is not much new to say about it; but it is an extremely serious subject for all who love their country, for the evil has been growing till it has reached a point where no further growth seems possible, since it is now almost universal.

I once asked a prison chaplain what class of criminals he found most irreclaimable. I did not expect him to name the murderers, for a man may commit a murder under sudden provocation, without being altogether a bad character. I thought he might have chosen pickpockets or blackmailers. But he answered without hesitation, "The gamblers."

This gives food for reflection, when we look at the headlines and posters for our evening papers. Racing, which means betting, for most of the readers of newspapers know and care nothing about horses, takes precedence of every other topic, unless the editors are able to report a "sensational collapse of England," which, as a foreigner would learn with surprise, and probably with disappointment, means only that the Australian bowlers have been on the spot. Betting and gambling—we need not distinguish between them—are now the chief national vice of this country, far more widespread than alcoholic intemperance.

Some people, of course, say that there is nothing wrong in moderate betting, any more than in moderate drinking.   It is this opinion that I propose to examine.

Betting or gambling has been defined as the determination of the ownership of property by an appeal to chance.   There may be no such thing as chance, but we may give the name to a play of natural forces which cannot be controlled or calculated by those who appeal to it.   Pure gambling is an appeal to pure chance; to toss a coin is the simplest example. Mixed gambling contains an element of skill or of fraud.   To bet on a certainty is, of course, pure fraud.   To buy a speculative stock is mixed gambling, because we act partly from confidence in our own judgment, and partly because we are willing to run a considerable risk.   If I insure my life, I am betting on the chances of my own early decease; it is often worth while to do this, because those who are dependent on me, so far as they have any choice in the matter, may be said to have speculated on my being able to earn my living till old age. To play at a gaming table is pure gambling, with gratuitous folly added, because the players know that a percentage on the stakes is levied by the establishment.

The mention of insurance, and of risky investments, shows how difficult the problem is. Economists say that a high rate of interest is partly interest and partly insurance, and that no business can be carried on without some degree of speculation. Probably no business man could draw a sharp line between legitimate and illegitimate speculation, and certainly no one else could.

There are some people who cannot enjoy a game of cards unless they are playing for money. If the players are equal in skill, and play frequently for the same stakes, they are not likely to have gained or lost much at the end of the year. Are we to blame them or not? Personally, I always refuse to play for money, but that may be because it would give me no pleasure to win and a great deal of annoyance to lose.

I suppose the chief cause of betting and gambling is a rebellion against the monotony of ordinary life. The world offers most of us nothing but a repetition of the same drudgery, with petty rewards which are all known beforehand. A margin of disorder, of the incalculable, adds to the interest of living. The Asiatic dislikes our taxation, not because it is oppressive but because it is regular. There is nothing sporting about a half-yearly demand note; but there is something exciting in the doubt whether the Rajah will swoop upon our hen-roosts this year, or whether we shall escape being taxed altogether. So some of us amuse ourselves, as Charles Lamb did, by reading the Restoration dramatists, and "imagining ourselves in a world with no meddling moral distinctions." Betting, in fact, is a relief from boredom; those who are lucky enough to have made their work their play seldom feel any temptation to gamble. Those who either hate their work, or who have no work to do, almost all yield to the temptation.

The gambling spirit is very bad for a nation, because it repudiates the rational basis of acquisition, which is the natural relation of effort to satisfaction. Wealth would not be produced but for the satisfaction of consuming it, and the use of it ought to be the reward for some social service. There is much unjust distribution, but even this is better than mere chance. Property honestly earned is respectable; but property acquired by chance or fraud has no sacredness. This is one reason why attacks on property always follow great wars. The gambling profiteer is too much in evidence, and to fleece him seems no robbery.   He has done too well for himself, while others risked their lives.

The tree is known by its fruits, and the fruits of betting and gambling are wholly bad.   The gambler frequently defrauds his creditors, leaves his family ruined, and tries to repair by fraud what he has lost by chance.   There are habitual gamblers, who are as much slaves to their besetting sin as any opium-eater.   I have only once been inside the Casino at Monte Carlo.   It is a spot where "every prospect pleases," but it seemed to me that "man" looked decidedly "vile," and woman much viler. To live in this sort of artificial excitement must be very bad for the character.

The proposal to tax betting was objected to mainly by the working man, who saw in it a scheme to tax his pleasures, a thing not to be thought of.   But it was censured also by many moralists, on the ground that the State ought not to make money out of vice. Assuming that the money must be raised somehow, I would much rather see it collected by taxing vice, in the persons of bookmakers and their clients, than by taxing virtue in the person of myself.   To say that we do not "recognise" betting is rather silly; we cannot help reading the newspaper posters.   It is this sort of argument which makes foreigners call us hypocrites.

But the real seriousness of betting and gambling is realised only when we consider of what mental condition they are symptomatic. An utter lack of intelligent interests, a dreary boredom and discontent, an entire want of conscience about the getting and spending of money—these are the only states of mind that could drive anyone to the gaming table or the sporting columns of the newspapers. To the man who has found his vocation this gadfly of boredom and monotony is unknown. When the educated man wants to unstring his bow, there are a dozen more interesting employments of his leisure hours waiting for him.

The evil may probably be attacked most successfully from the intellectual rather than from the moral side. This kind goeth not out, save by education and intelligent interests. It is a disease of barbarians, superficially civilised. These are the people who are always in search of excitement, and who plunge into one folly after another to escape the spectre of boredom, which after all they can never escape, because they are bored by their own emptyheadedness.

1924.

XIII

SCHOOLBOY STORIES

THOSE who have studied public school magazines will have been struck both by the excellence of the English verse compositions, and by the heaviness of the sixth-form boy when he tries to be humorous. He gambols like a tame elephant. But when the human boy does not wish to be funny, he is sometimes inimitable. When I was a schoolmaster, I made a collection of the unconscious *bons mots* of my pupils, and of others which my colleagues told me, and I have added to it since from hearsay.

Some of these stories may very likely have become "chestnuts"; others, I hope, will be new to my readers. It is a very frivolous subject, after the serious problems which I have been discussing week by week; but I feel that I owe my readers a laugh.

Theology is a subject in which profane jesting is doubtless out of place. But the schoolboy's blunders are too innocent to offend anybody. It was an ordination candidate, not a schoolboy, who hoped to conciliate an orthodox bishop by writing down, "I believe in all things, both visible and invisible"—all that he could remember of the Nicene Creed. Another would-be pillar of the Church informed his examiners that "the youthful Origen declared his intention of going out to seek martyrdom. His father saved him by hiding his trousers." It was an Oxford undergraduate who, when asked, in his *viva voce*, to say what he knew of Joab, replied "Joab was a wash-pot."

But the genuine schoolboy can do better. One of them wrote: "The Pharisees were a very mean and stingy lot. One of them brought a penny to our Lord, who, when he had looked at it, said 'Whose *subscription* is this?'" A young Etonian, whose papers I read, was asked, "What are the essentials of a Sacrament, according to the Church of England? Show that the other so-called Sacraments do not fulfil the conditions." He wrote: "The essentials of a Sacrament are Faith and Repentance. Hence it follows that matrimony cannot be a sacrament." He differed, apparently, from the boy who wrote: "Christians are only allowed one wife. This is called monotony."

We are all anxious to find our own opinions in authoritative documents, and critics have performed many acrobatic feats of interpretation with this object. A few years ago some of our bishops proposed to "retranslate" the Athanasian Creed, in a

way which would remove all stumbling-blocks from
the minds of the laity. The new version was to
begin, "Whoever wishes to be spiritually healthy."
This was plucky, but a still bolder "retranslation"
was made by a small fourth-form pupil of mine at
Eton. "If any man shall smite thee on the right
cheek, smite him on the other also." Thus the
Sermon on the Mount was triumphantly brought into
complete harmony with schoolboy ethics. The boy
who referred, "First the blade, then the ear" to
St. Peter and Malchus was rather ingenious. An
unkind remark was once made in an examination
that "Some of the best fossils are found in theological cabinets."

History, as told by the schoolboy, contains some
surprising facts. "The isles of Greece were always
quarrelling about the birthplace of Homer. Chaos
has the best right to claim him." "Luther is famous
for his Diet of Worms. At last he said, Heaven
help me! I can take no other course." The schoolboy is great on "last words," but some of his master-
pieces, like the last words of Oliver Cromwell, "If I
had served my God," etc., are common property.
Dr. Butler, of Harrow, had a sentimental reverence
for Charles I. Once he asked a boy, with tears in
his voice, "And what were the last words of the Royal
martyr?" (It will be recollected that the right

answer was "Remember, Juxon"—a mysterious reminder to the Bishop who attended him on the scaffold; and also that Charles II.'s last thoughts were for Nell Gwyn: "Don't let poor Nelly starve.") The boy put the two together, and answered, "Remember Juxon; don't let poor Juxon starve."

Many years ago a little book appeared called *Very Original English*—it is probably forgotten by this time. The editor was an elementary schoolmaster, who culled gems from the essays of his little pupils. We read in it how "Jacob was a patriarch, who brought up his twelve sons to be patriarchs, but they did not take to it. Jacob didn't eat much as a rule, except when there was a famine in the land." (Perverse old man!) Another essay, with very original spelling, gives us some facts about The Cat. "A cat is a quadruped, the legs as usual being at the four corners. Do not tease cats; for firstly it is wrong so to do, and secondly kittens has clawses, which is longer than people thinks. Cats has nine liveses, but which is seldom required in this country, cos of Christianity."

The "General Paper," that rather absurd institution which in reality is more easily "crammed" than any other, brings occasional mirth to the examiner. "Ammonia is the food of the gods." "Ipe-

· ac is a man who likes a good dinner." "A dema-
ᴌ ᴣue is a vessel containing beer and other liquids."
"Guerrilla warfare was when men rode on gorillas."
"The Test Act was passed to keep Roman Catholics out of public-houses." "An interval in music
is the distance from one piano to the next."

Mathematicians are not supposed to lend themselves much to humour, but we must congratulate
the youths who said that "geometry teaches us how
to bisex angels," and that "an angle is a triangle with
only two sides." But perhaps the best achievement in this subject was the answer to a question
about the difference between Problems and Theo-
rems in Euclid. "A Problem may be solved by
merely human intelligence; but a Theorem (derived
from *Theos*, 'God,' and *res*, 'a thing') requires the
Divine assistance."

Elementary science provides unlimited opportunities for the unconscious jester. Defective hearing
is probably responsible for the definition of the equa-
tor as a "menagerie lion running round the middle
of the globe." And here I may say that Sunday-
school children often miss the edifying lessons contained in hymns by mishearing the words. A whole
class in London were supposed to be repeating

> Thou did'st here obedience show;
> O make me obedient too.

But the Cockney accent of the teacher misled them,
and what they actually said was:

> Thou did'st here a pigeon show;
> O make me a pigeon too.

No one will dispute that "if the air contains more
than 100 per cent. of carbolic acid, it is very injuri-
ous to health." The Papal Court is doubtless less
busy than it used to be, but "a vacuum is a large
empty space where the Pope lives," sounds like an
exaggeration.

We turn to the French language. Probably many
boys have hit on the obvious derivation of *dimanche:*
"Because you eat twice as much on that day as on
week-days." *Hors de combat*, "a charger"; *chevaux
de frise*, "a shivering fit"; *cordon bleu*, "a teeto-
taller," all have their merits. But how sure the boy
must have felt that he was right when he explained
the proverb *Le jeu ne vaut pas la chandelle*, "The
Jew is not worth the scandal. This is what the
French said when they refused to let poor Captain
Dreyfus out of prison." Truly pathetic is the pro-
verbial philosophy of the youth who, with poignant
memories of a painful interview with the headmaster, translated *Tout vient à point à qui sait
attendre*, "Everything comes to a point to him whose
seat is tender."

Many of the best jokes are in translation from, or composition in, Latin and Greek. But in these degenerate days it is to be feared that only a minority of my readers would see the fun of them. The boy who derived "sermon" from *sero moneo*, "I warn too late," knew something of the world. Many schoolmasters have laughed over the ingenious rendering of "We thought her dying when she slept, And sleeping when she died." *"Dormiens virgo moriens videtur, Et vice versa,"* though here the schoolmaster was in fault for setting such an impossible metre for the translation. It was, of course, a young lady pupil who translated *Ad unguem factus homo* "The young man was brought to the scratch."

Dr. Hornby, of Eton, was fond of quoting a translation of Horace's *Crescentem sequitur cura pecuniam, maiorumque fames*, "Increase of money is followed by care, and by a hunger for ancestors." "Burke's Peerage" and "Landed Gentry," he said, amply confirmed this statement. It is not often that so many howlers can be got into one line as by the boy who translated *Vis consili expers mole ruit sua*, "The unexpected weight of the consul fell upon the soft pig." It is a pleasant picture, and worth a whipping.

A stranger sends me some additional gems.

"Charon was a man who fried soles over the sticks."

"The Duke of Marlborough was a great general. He always fought with the fixed determination to win or lose."

"To keep milk from turning sour you should keep it in the cow."

"On one side of a penny is the King's head, on the other a young lady riding a bicycle: they call her Ruby Tanyer."

"Contralto is a low sort of music which only ladies sing."

"Simon de Montfort formed what was known as the Mad Parliament. It was something the same as it is at the present day."

"The name of Cæsar's wife was Cæsarea; she was above suspicion."

"Socrates died from an overdose of wedlock."

1920.

IV
Religious

I

THE LAMBETH CONFERENCE

(I)

THE report of the Lambeth Conference has now been published. It is impossible to read the list of dioceses represented at this great gathering without a sense of pride at the world-wide diffusion of the British race, and a very deep thankfulness that the issue of the Great War has left our vast Empire still intact and able to send its representatives to London as fellow-citizens of one mighty Commonwealth. The Conference had almost the dignity of an Ecumenical Council.

Nevertheless, there were grounds for anxiety about the results of its deliberations. The majority of the Bishops representing Overseas dioceses have not a very high average of intellectual distinction, and the American Episcopal Church, which sent so large a contingent, is numerically a small sect, in which a good private income is an almost indispensable qualification for a bishopric.

There are also stumbling-blocks peculiar to an

Episcopal conclave.   Bishop Phillips Brooks, something of an *enfant terrible* on the bench, wrote: "The bishops are not very wise, nor very clever; but they think they are, and they very much enjoy being bishops."   The high theory of the Episcopate now popular among the bishops obliges them to claim a sort of inspiration, forgetful of Selden's irreverent gibe that in Church Councils "the odd man is the Holy Ghost."

But in Lambeth Conferences the decision is seldom left to the odd man.   The danger is that a small, uncompromising faction, reckless whether they upset the coach or not, may impose its will on the majority, who dread nothing so much as a secession, threats of which were freely brandished over their heads at the last Decennial Conference, held, if I remember right, in 1908.

In these two articles it will be possible only to comment on some of the resolutions and reports, selecting those which are most important in themselves and likely to be of most interest to the public at large.

The nation was prepared for some definite constructive proposals to help forward the reunion of the separated religious bodies.   It is widely recognised that many of these divisions no longer correspond to any real differences in religious faith; not that such differences do not exist, but that the various types of religious conviction, which are mainly determined by differences of temperament, are all represented in every large denomination.

Secessions occur on points of principle, but schisms are continued without any justification, and become more unreasonable in each succeeding generation. The experience of soldiers at the front certainly added to the impatience against sectarianism, which had long been felt among the laity, who were aware of the dangerous tendencies which threaten impartially every form of Christian belief and Christian practice.

The Conference was not ignorant of this widespread impatience, and its members approached the problem with a due sense of its urgency. A real step forward has been taken by the resolution on page 26 of the report:—

We acknowledge all those who believe in our Lord Jesus Christ, and have been baptised into the name of the Holy Trinity, as sharing with us membership in the universal Church of Christ which is His Body.

And on page 28:—

We thankfully acknowledge that these ministries (of non-episcopal bodies) have been manifestly blessed and owned by the Holy Spirit as effective means of grace.

The following practical directions to bishops will also be welcomed as valuable steps towards the recognition of the status of other denominations:—

A bishop is justified in giving occasional authorisation to ministers not episcopally ordained who, in his judgment, are working towards an ideal of union such as is set forth in our appeal, to preach in churches within his diocese, and to clergy of the diocese to preach in churches of such ministers. The bishops of the Anglican Communion will not question the action of any bishop who, in the few years between the invitation and completion of a definite scheme of union, shall countenance the irregularity of admitting to communion the baptised but unconfirmed communicants of non-episcopal congregations concerned in this scheme.

Two more important resolutions follow:—

(i) Nothing in these resolutions is intended to indicate that the rule of confirmation as conditioning admission to the Holy Communion must necessarily apply to the case of baptised persons who seek communion under conditions which in the bishop's judgment justify their admission thereto.

(ii) In cases in which it is impossible for the bishop's judgment to be obtained beforehand the priest should remember that he has no canonical authority to refuse communion to any baptised person kneeling before the Lord's Table (unless he be excommunicate by name, or in the canonical sense of the term a cause of scandal to the faithful); and that if a question may properly be raised as to the future admission of any such person to Holy Communion, either because he has not been confirmed or for other reasons, the priest should refer the matter to the bishop for counsel or direction.

The conditions of reunion, as laid down by the Bishops, are acceptance of the Holy Scriptures, the Nicene Creed, and the two Sacraments. But there is unfortunately a fourth condition, the acceptance of episcopacy. So uncompromising is the Conference in asserting a difference of status between those Churches which are episcopally governed and those which are not, that the Bishops will accept without any demur complete mutual recognition between the Anglican Church and the Orthodox Eastern Churches, in spite of their refusal to admit a clause in our Nicene Creed, and "closer relations" with the separated Churches of the East, if they can give "satisfactory assurances as to their faith." They will also admit members of the Swedish Church, which is an episcopal body, to Communion.

On the other hand, they propose that ministers

of the English Nonconformist bodies, and of the Scottish Presbyterians, should submit to episcopal ordination as a condition of reunion with the Church of England. In return, they "would willingly accept from these authorities a form of commission or recognition which would commend our ministry to their congregations, as having its place in the one family life." They evidently consider this as a handsome offer, and hope that it may be accepted.

I fear, however, that this policy virtually cuts off the hope of reunion with the Scottish Presbyterians, who are far nearer to the Church of England than, for instance, the Russian Church. There is a very small number of Presbyterian ministers who might fall in with the Bishops' scheme, and I have reason to think that these have misled some of the leaders of the Church of England into supposing that there is a strong body of opinion behind them. My information is that this is far from being true. The vast majority would almost indignantly refuse to submit to a ceremony which, in spite of protestations to the contrary, would seem to them to imply a defect in their own commissions. The whole history of Presbyterianism forbids us to expect any other attitude.

The almost superstitious glorification of the episcopal office. which lies at the bottom of this proposal, depends mainly on a mere legend, the "apostolic succession"; but human nature may be credited with some disposition on the part of the Bishops to magnify their office. Five weeks of close deliberation may have somewhat shaken their faith in one another's infallibility, but the mystical theory of the episcopate has manifestly determined their policy towards schemes of reunion. Nevertheless, a step forward has been taken, and it is right to welcome with gratitude the signs of a more liberal temper and a more genuine desire to find some practical way to heal the wounds of Christendom than has before found expression in an episcopal pronouncement.

THE MINISTRY OF WOMEN

The conference is to be congratulated on being willing to move with the times in recognising the altered status of women. Women are henceforth to be allowed to do everything that laymen may do. They are to be ordained, if they wish it, as deaconesses, and permitted to administer baptism in case of necessity. (The traditional doctrine, I believe, is that baptism by a woman is valid, but that "it ought not to be done.") They are to be allowed, with the approval of the bishop and incumbent, to read the prayers and give addresses in church at the regular services. This last resolution was only carried by

117 votes to 81.   But no objection, it appears, was
made to allowing extra services to be conducted by
women in church.

This policy is a really courageous innovation,
which I have no doubt will be completely justified
by its results.   The full admission of women to the
priesthood may come later; but it would not be
practicable at present, and there is no reason to
think that any large number of women desire it.

SPIRITUALISM, CHRISTIAN SCIENCE, THEOSOPHY

The strange recrudescence of superstition in England, which the war has greatly stimulated, seemed
to the Bishops to necessitate a pronouncement on
these subjects.   The resolutions are wise and tem-
perately worded.   The only criticism that might be
made upon them is that they are too respectful in
tone; but the Bishops doubtless remembered that
many otherwise sensible persons have been carried
away by these enchantments, the love of which is
deeply rooted in human nature.

II

THE LAMBETH CONFERENCE

(II)

Divorce

THAT part of the report of the Lambeth Conference which relates to problems of marriage and sexual morality is undoubtedly the poorest and least satisfactory portion of the whole document; it will cause general disappointment. The report of the committee is written in an unbalanced rhetorical style which compares unfavourably with the reports of the other committees, and is particularly unfortunate in dealing with a delicate subject on which the public is still badly informed, and on which calm wisdom and adequate knowledge are called for.

The question of divorce is just now so urgent that a much fuller elucidation of principles would have been desirable. The bishops refuse even to consider the extension of the grounds of divorce to other grave offences besides adultery, on the ground that the words of Christ have decided the question for all time.

But many good authorities think it unlikely that our Lord intended on this occasion to abandon His usual practice of refusing to legislate; and considering the uncertainty which hangs over that particular passage in the Gospel, and that different churches have adopted different interpretations to guide their own practice, it is certain that many loyal Christians will be unwilling to accept a simple *non possumus*, as precluding all further discussion of a most difficult question.

REMARRIAGE OF THE INNOCENT

There is another point which ought to have been cleared up. Certain High Church bishops have instructed their clergy, as a matter of obedience to themselves, to refuse to allow the remarriage of the innocent party in a divorce case to be celebrated in church, and even to refuse to read the banns.

This is, of course, flagrantly illegal. It is part of a new claim by the bishops to override the law of the land and to establish an autocracy, which will hardly commend itself to the more democratically organised bodies to which they are offering terms of reunion. The whole subject of divorce bristles with difficulties, and may even produce a situation in-

compatible with the maintenance of the Establishment. There is no evidence that the Committee of
Bishops weighed the problem with the thoroughness
which might have been expected.

BIRTH CONTROL

Another difficult problem which came before this
committee is the very delicate subject of birth-
control. It is notorious that various causes, among
which the sharp decline in the infant death rate is not
the least important, have made it necessary for
nearly all married people to restrict the number of
their children, in order that they may do their best
for those children who are born. This restriction is
naturally not made the subject of conversation, but
everyone knows that it is almost universal, except
among the reckless and degraded population of the
slums; and only a few very foolish persons think
that it is either immoral or regrettable.

The resulting fall of about 35 per cent. in the
birth rate, which has accompanied an almost exactly
parallel fall in the death rate, still leaves an ample
margin of increase, amounting to nine or ten per
thousand a year. This voluntary limitation of
births is most marked in the learned professions,
who are finding it increasingly difficult to keep up a
decent standard of living in the face of crushing

taxation and inelastic incomes. Next to the doctors and the teaching professions, the clergy are now
foremost in exercising the necessary prudence.

Eugenists are right to deplore a social system
which imposes the heaviest burdens on a class which
may claim to be the physical and intellectual élite
of the community; but while those conditions remain,
it is useless to blame the victims of them for taking
the course which is obviously best for their children.

In spite of these facts, which are well known to
everybody, the bishops speak of birth-control as a
practice hostile to the family, and the committee
declares, in its curious phraseology, that the lowered birth rate "sounds a note of serious alarm and
warning." The committee expresses the opinion
that no means of limiting the family is justifiable
except the complete cessation of marital relations
between husband and wife. In this case it is impossible to acquit the married bishops, who must
know the truth about wedded life, of want of can-
dour and courage in recognising facts which, though
they are not talked about, are matters of common
knowledge.

There are, it is true, some couples who even in
the prime of life are capable of the dissolution of
marriage on its physical side, which the bishops
recommend; but in the large majority of cases such

counsel either cannot be followed, or can only be followed at the cost of impairing the harmony of married life and the peace of mind of one or both parties. It is simply untrue to say that this is a sensual view of marriage; it is merely an honest recognition of human nature as it is.

The only result of this report can be to trouble the consciences of many persons whose own hearts do not condemn them. It was a grave blunder to put celibate bishops in a prominent position on this committee.

SOCIAL AND INDUSTRIAL QUESTIONS

I approached the perusal of this section with alarm, and finished it with relief. After my experience of many recent ecclesiastical utterances, I expected a profession of a vague and sentimental socialism, intended to impress the class who call themselves the workers with the assurance that the Church is their ally. The present excesses of the trade unions have no doubt opened the eyes of the public to their real aims, and have imposed modera· tion upon the Bishops in council. The Conference does not talk about "the suffering and toiling masses," a favourite phrase in the past, which is hardly suitable to the bricklayer who battens on

the rates and does about two and a half hours of
honest work in the day.

The resolution wisely and courageously calls
attention to the moral source of our social unhappi-
ness. "A fundamental change in the spirit and
working of our economic life" is required. The
principle of co-operation for the common good must
take the place of competition for private or sectional
advantage. The Church cannot be "a judge or a
divider" in political or class disputes; its duty is to
uphold "the equal value of every human personality"; and the obligation "of avoiding extrav-
agance and waste, and of upholding a high standard
of honour and thoroughness in work."

The report, which goes more into detail, has the
courage to stigmatise limitation of output as "a
disastrous fallacy." On the whole, this Committee, which included among its chief members
some men of revolutionary leanings, may be congratulated on a report characterised by sanity and
fair-mindedness, and thoroughly Christian in tone
and temper.

Alcohol

The Bishops seem favourably disposed towards
the prohibition of alcohol; but they do not commit
themselves to support of legislation with this object.

They call attention to the really alarming expenditure on strong drink in 1919, thereby inviting us
to consider whether a nation which spends nearly
four hundred million pounds a year in drink can
hope to compete successfully with a nation which
spends nothing.

THE LEAGUE OF NATIONS

It was to be expected that the conference should
express entire sympathy with the League of Nations. At the present time moral support is almost
all that we can give, and the Conference has given
this support in well-chosen language. We may note
with great satisfaction that the American and
Colonial Bishops accepted the following resolution,
which is printed on page 26: "The conference records
its protest against the colour-prejudice among the
different races of the world, which not only hinders
intercourse, but gravely imperils the peace of the
future."

MODERNISM

Lastly, we must call attention to one remarkable
omission in the report. It contains no doctrinal
statement and no anathemas against Modernism.
It is difficult not to hazard a guess that we owe this
omission to the wisdom of the Primate and some of

his chief coadjutors. The Bishops have consented not to play the part of King Canute once more, and we may be very thankful for their decision.

Conclusion

Some may be doubtful whether these results are sufficient to justify the assembling of 250 Bishops from all parts of the earth, and taking them away from their dioceses for so long a time. But the Conference has probably had a valuable educative effect on many whose sphere of work lies far from the centres of thought; it has, we may hope, cemented the friendship between Britain and the United States, on which so much depends; it has emphasised and strengthened the unity of the whole Anglican communion; and it has done its work without any rupture between the parties in the Church.

Some disappointments were inevitable, and probably no party in the Church is wholly satisfied; but those who know the difficulties and pitfalls which lay in the path of the Conference will probably conclude that it has been very successful, and will share the gratitude which the members expressed to the President and his secretaries, on whom the general management of the Conference devolved.

1920.

III

REUNION IN GREAT BRITAIN

THE desire for a reunion of the Christian churches, now so often expressed, gives rise to strange reflections. To the historian it does not seem very long since men and women in tens of thousands submitted to be imprisoned, tortured, hanged, and burnt alive, sooner than make their submission to the Great Church in which they saw embodied the spirit of Anti-christ. The wars of religion caused the deaths of two-thirds of the population of Germany. Thousands of English people accepted banishment from their homes, and faced the dangers of the wilderness and the scalping-knife of the savage, in order that they might be free to worship God according to their consciences. Thousands of Frenchmen, after the revocation of the Edict of Nantes, fled to this country, enriching its population with a stock as bold, energetic, and intelligent as that which England had lost with the Pilgrim Fathers. British Nonconformists endured many disabilities, such as exclusion from the universities, rather than make their peace with the Church of England.

Have the conditions changed? Are the causes which then justified secession and the endurance of cruel persecution no longer operative? Do the dissentients no longer believe what they believed three hundred years ago? Or is the Great Church more tolerant and less tyrannical than it was when they left her? These are questions which must be answered if we are to decide whether the movement toward reunion has any strength behind it.

Is the desire for the fusion of religious bodies at all widespread? The Church of Rome stands by itself and must be considered separately. But how does the matter stand in the Reformed churches?

In Scotland the subdivisions of the Presbyterians are felt to be unnecessary and undesirable. Reunion among them may soon be an accomplished fact. There are no doctrinal differences such as could be thought to justify the inconvenience of rival organisations in the same village. Similarly, the English and Welsh Nonconformists, or Free Churchmen, as they call themselves, acknowledge that the fissiparous tendency which has called into being scores of little sects, teaching much the same things, is an absurdity. There has been some fusion, and a general friendliness and mutual recognition. The political decay of the middle class, to which most of their adherents belong, has diminished their prestige and their resources. Amalgamation is being almost forced upon them.

The Established Church of England is the most divided body in Christendom. The majority of its members stand aloof from the Nonconformists, with some slight trace of the old social disdain, and have no desire whatever for reconciliation with Rome. But ever since the Tractarian movement of Queen Victoria's reign there has been an active body of Anglo-Catholics who dislike the word Protestant, and seek to introduce into the Church of England the greater part of the Roman doctrine and practice. They are a comparatively weak minority among the laity and strong among the clergy. Being energetic and enthusiastic, with a great aptitude for corporate action, they have become the dominant party in our church councils, and by capturing most of the clergy training colleges they can bring pressure to bear upon the episcopate.

It is from this party that the overtures for reunion with continental Catholicism have proceeded. They have endeavoured to establish friendly relations with the Orthodox Eastern Church, and these efforts have been reciprocated. Eastern prelates have attended our cathedral services in their robes, and have preached in our pulpits. In my own Cathedral we have welcomed a Serbian bishop, the Archbishop of

Cyprus, and the Archbishop of Athens. The last-named gave the benediction at my request at a Sunday service in St. Paul's. These overtures have the sympathy of almost all Anglicans, just because there can be no question of amalgamating the two churches, but only of mutual recognition and inter-communion.

Very different has been the fate of conversations with the Roman Church. The rigid exclusiveness of that church is a fixed policy from which there is neither the will nor the power to deviate. From the Roman Catholic point of view, the Reformed churches are simply revolted subjects, who can be restored to favour only in return for absolute sub-mission. There has never been the slightest doubt on this point, and the overtures of Lord Halifax and his friends have been both foolish and humiliat-ing. The conversations at Malines had no import-ance in themselves, and Cardinal Mercier lost no time in explaining that he consented to them only in the hope of bringing wandering sheep back to the fold. The attention which the conference attracted was simply due to the fact that the Archbishop of Canterbury, who has a well-earned reputation for prudence and caution, seems to have been misled into supposing that the Vatican was interested in the matter. The incident has done no harm; it has served to clear the air, and to demonstrate the utter futility of seeking reconciliation with Rome. If such a thing were possible, which happily it is not, it would split the Church of England from top to bottom. The men who suffered for their faith in Queen Mary's reign were not more determined than many Anglicans to-day, to have no dealings with the priestly Cæsar in the Vatican.

We cannot pass a sponge over the history of the Church of England for the last 350 years. In spite of some mistakes, it has been a chapter of English history in which we may take an honest pride. We do not regret the Reformation, and we will not dis-own the long line of Anglican saints, divines, and statesmen who have helped to mould the character of our people. We value our independence and we will keep it. Unity in Christ with our spiritual kith and kin abroad is one thing; any hint of submission to a foreign Church is another. The former we will seek to promote; the latter we will resist and stead-fastly refuse.

Meanwhile, reunion with another church, that of Sweden, has been practically recognised. Eng-lish bishops have taken part in the consecration of a Swedish bishop, and very friendly relations have been established.

To most Englishmen the question of reunion at

home is far more important than recognition by foreign churches. But here the Lambeth Conference seems to have missed a great opportunity. The comradeship of the trenches, and the experience of a great national danger shared in common, had predisposed Britons of all denominations to draw together in fellowship. There had been much fraternising at the front; and the soldiers felt that the High Anglican theory, which divides all other Christians into those who unchurch them and those whom they unchurch, was not only uncharitable but ridiculous. There was very little wish among Free Churchmen for incorporation in the Established Church, but there was a strong desire for a recognition by Anglicans of the validity of their ministries, and for such acts of unity as occasional interchange of pulpits and occasional intercommunion. Unfortunately the bishops, who were above all things anxious to prevent an Anglo-Catholic secession, misunderstood the situation, and, instead of sanctioning acts of unity, proposed a scheme by which the Free Church ministers might be recognised as priests and deacons of the Anglican Church, if they would consent to reordination. The proposal was doomed to failure from the start; polite language has been used on both sides, but nothing effective has been done, or ever can be done, on those lines. The aggressive activity of the Anglo-Catholic party has diminished the desire—which was never felt by many Nonconformists—to enter into closer legal relations with the Anglicans. In a word, they desire recognition and fellowship; they do not desire incorporation.

So the matter stands in this country. There is an insuperable barrier between Rome and all the Reformed churches. There is a barrier, hitherto unsurmounted, between the Anglican Church and Nonconformity. There are no other important obstacles to friendly co-operation, except that the more orthodox bodies have difficulties about accepting the Unitarians on doctrinal grounds, and the Quakers on account of their repudiation of Sacraments.

The question remains to be answered—Why is the ideal of an external, political reunion of Christendom attractive to many? There is no doubt that the words "that they all may be one"—*ut omnes unum sint*—evoke strong and wistful aspirations in many minds. But it is only in the Vulgate, not in the Greek text, that Christ prays that his disciples may all be penned in "one fold." He really speaks of "one flock." There are other kinds of unity besides institutional union.

The political unity of the Church is an idea which

belongs to the Middle Ages. It is the counterpart of the idea of a universal empire. Both had their focus in the majesty of the name of Rome. "The analogy of the two," Lord Bryce says, "made them appear parts of one great world-movement toward unity; the coincidence of their boundaries, which had begun before Constantine, lasted long enough after him to associate them indissolubly together, and make the names of Roman and Christian convertible." After the fall of the secular empire, "the whole fabric of mediæval Christianity rested upon the idea of the visible Church. Such a church could be in nowise local or limited."

We have, therefore, an adequate historical explanation of the idea of a politically united Christendom. It belongs to the same political philosophy as the theory that there could be only one Empire. Even the Turkish Sultans have been known to claim that the Roman Empire survived in their persons. The Roman Church has never hesitated to claim universal spiritual sovereignty. The New World was conquered for the Pope no less than for the King of Spain.

But we have no sooner traced the origin of this idea than we realise what an utter anachronism it is. A universal empire is forever impossible, not only because no nation is strong enough to conquer the whole earth, but because the independent nations have a strong individuality, which would make it impossible for them to form parts of a single political aggregate. Even small provinces offer a stubborn and usually successful resistance to alien domination. This intense consciousness of nationality belongs on the whole to modern history. The Roman steamroller obliterated nationalities or prevented their growth, and in the chaos of the Dark Ages there was no opportunity for nations to develop their distinctive characters. The conditions favoured not only the fact of a spiritual empire, but the peculiar philosophy which justified it. This philosophy has been summed up by Lord Bryce: "Humanity is an essential quality present in all men, and making them what they are. The whole truth of their being lies in the universal property, which alone has a permanent and independent existence. The common nature of the individuals thus gathered into one Being is typified in its two aspects, the spiritual and the secular, by two persons, the World-Priest and the World-Monarch, who present on earth a similitude of the Divine unity."

The beginning of the modern period brought to a final end the possibility of a universal Church. The Latin and Greek parts of Europe had separated already, and at the Reformation the Nordic and the Mediterranean races settled on a divorce. Latin Christianity was henceforth the Christianity of the Latin nations. To suppose that these cleavages, following, as they do, well-marked racial lines, will ever be joined together, is a dream. Of my own nation Professor Santayana says: "If the Englishman likes to call himself a Catholic, it is a fad, like a thousand others, to which his inner man, so seriously playful, is prone to lend itself. He may go over to Rome on a spiritual tour; but if he is converted really and becomes a Catholic at heart, he is no longer the man he was. Words cannot measure the chasm which must henceforth separate him from everything at home. For a modern Englishman, with freedom and experiment and reserve in his blood, to go over to Rome is essential suicide; the inner man must succumb first. Such an Englishman might become a saint, but only by becoming a foreigner."

The upshot of all this is that the institutional unification which some desire is neither practicable nor desirable. An independent nation must be independent in the spiritual as well as in the secular sphere. It will so best make its proper contribution to the spiritual commonwealth, displaying that hue of the "many-coloured wisdom of God" (as St. Paul says) which Divine providence ordained that it should bring to perfection. The unity of Christendom which alone we can desire and rationally seek to promote is not the unity of a world-wide centralised government, but unity of spirit based on a common faith and a common desire to see the Kingdom of God, which is "righteousness and peace and joy in the Holy Ghost," established on earth. There will be diversities of gifts, but the same Spirit; differences of ecclesiastical organisation, but the same Lord. We must not expect that India, China, and Japan, if they ever adopt Christianity, will be European Christians. They have their ancient traditions, unlike the Græco-Roman traditions which formed Catholicism; they must build their national churches upon these, in complete independence.

The sole bond of a spiritually united Christendom is the Person and the Gospel of the Divine Founder.

1924.

IV

RELIGION IN ENGLAND AFTER THE WAR

In England as in America the question is frequently asked, How has the Great War affected the
religion of the people? An honest answer, though
probably a superficial one, would be that to all
appearance it has made no difference at all. Take
the most obvious and least satisfactory of all tests,
that of attendance at public worship. In my
cathedral, and in most of the other London churches,
the congregations are neither larger nor smaller than
they were at the beginning of 1914. During the
first months of the war they seemed to be rather
larger; then, owing to the absence of the younger
men on military service, and the absorption of many
others in various kinds of war work, they were somewhat below the average; now they are just where
they were before the war. The amount of money
subscribed to religious institutions, and in support of
appeals for religious objects, has neither increased
nor diminished to any appreciable extent. Interest
in religious questions is keen, as it always is in

England, but it does not seem to have been diverted into any new channel.

We have listened with respect to the reports of chaplains who served with the forces, because we knew that the British soldier in this war was no longer Tommy Atkins, but the essential John Bull. But though the chaplains have been very ready to give their opinions, sometimes in very dogmatic language, their witness agrees not together. It has too plainly been biased by their preconceptions about religious truth and the office of the church. Some have reported that only sacramental religion and what they call Catholic teaching has any attraction for the soldier; they consider that the Roman Catholic priests have been more successful as padres than either Anglicans or Presbyterians. Others have emphasised the impatience felt by the soldiers at denominational prejudice and exclusiveness; they tell us that the army has discovered a common Christianity, and wishes for reunion all round. The best padres hesitate when they are asked whether the experience of war has made the average man more or less religious. They cannot say.

But it would not be right to omit one aspect in which the influence of the war upon belief may seem to have been wholly bad. At the outbreak of hostilities an able man made the prediction that the effect of the war would be to give a stimulus to the lower forms of religion, and to inflict a severe wound upon the higher kind of faith. For some years before the war there had been signs of a recrudescence of superstition, especially among the half-educated rich. This development was probably due in part to the growth of an anti-intellectualist philosophy and a revolt against the pretensions of natural science. The war undoubtedly stimulated this tendency. Soldiers are always prone both to fatalism and to superstition; many of our men are said to have carried amulets with them into action. At home there was a great outbreak of necromancy and spiritualism, which was supported by a few well-known men whose names gave authority to the movement. These men were themselves suffering from bereavement, and a large number of sorrowing parents and widows followed them in a pathetic endeavour to establish, by various forms of occultism, communion with the spirits of those whom they had dearly loved. It is difficult to decide whether these beliefs have taken deep root in the popular mind or not. The probability is that they will die down by degrees, except among a small number who are naturally attracted by anything strange, mysterious, and exciting.

The effect of the war upon moral conduct is also

difficult to estimate. An increase in sexual irregularities was to be expected, and there is no doubt that the desire to give soldiers on leave "a good time" led to many regrettable incidents. Some women who had lost their husbands contracted new ties with unfeeling levity. But, on the whole, the strain of the war was nobly borne, till it was over. Since the armistice, there has been much to grieve and shame any lover of his country. A new class of rich people has arisen, who took advantage of their country's necessities to make exorbitant profits, and who are now spending their ill-gotten gains with an ostentation as vulgar and tasteless as it is politically insane. A much larger class of workingmen, who were able, by threats of strikes, to obtain all that they asked for from the government, is showing a total absence of patriotic spirit by constantly increasing their demands, and by not even attempting to earn their pay. It is significant that the restriction of output is most scandalous in those trades where the workmen have the public at their mercy, and where no foreign competition is to be feared. The conduct of the bricklayers and some others is a national danger, the gravity of which can hardly be exaggerated. Meanwhile, those who had anything to lose in 1914 have mostly lost it. The whole burden of the war debt has been thrown on the few; the man with a fairly large fixed income, either from a professional office or from gilt-edged securities, finds his purchasing power reduced by nearly seventy-five per cent. The parochial clergy and others in similar positions are almost starving; and the prosperous artisan, who has been known to fill his parlor with a thousand-dollar piano (painted green by himself to match the rest of the furniture), will do nothing to help those upon whom he sponged in other days. Greed, selfishness, sloth, and materialism have never been so rampant as at present.

But jeremiads do no good, and it is unscientific to bring an indictment against a nation, or even against a class. We have to consider all the circumstances, and to give full weight to the effects of a reaction after unprecedented tension. It has seldom happened to any nation to be exposed without the slightest warning to so severe a physical and moral strain, and to be stretched on the rack without intermission for more than four years. In trying to understand the causes of our present frivolity and unrest, I recall to my thoughts the history of the last six years, the memory of which is branded indelibly on the minds of all who lived through them.

My first inkling of what was coming was on July 26, 1914, when a naval officer told me that a European war seemed to be inevitable, and that if it came we should not be able to keep out of it. From that day the sky began to darken. I went to Canterbury for the annual cricket-week, and assisted at the miserable attempts to carry through the customary socialities of that pleasant county gathering, till the storm broke and the holiday crowds melted away. At that time the feeling in England was that we had backed a bill for Belgium which we never expected to see presented, but which we were bound in honor to acknowledge. It was a horrible and utterly unforeseen misfortune, but we would show the Germans that as we had gone to war on the point of honour, we would fight them like chivalrous gentlemen and then shake hands. M. Chévrillon, whose brilliant little book, *L'Angleterre et la Guerre*, is an even truer picture of English psychology at that time than Mr. H. G. Wells's *Mr. Britling Sees It Through*, says that it took us some time to realise that a war with Germany was not a rather rough game of football. But the Germans made haste to undeceive us. The burning of Visé, the first Belgian town entered by the invaders, was a shock; the massacres at Termonde and elsewhere were hardly credited at first; the destruction of Louvain and of Rheims cathedral finally opened our eyes. But it was not till the bombardment of the undefended Yorkshire watering places, Whitby and Scarborough, the illegal use of

poison gas (which infuriated the soldiers more than
the outrages upon noncombatants), and above all
the *Lusitania* crime, that the whole nation blazed
out into fierce anger, the like of which only a few old
men could remember when in 1857 news came of the
massacre at Cawnpore.

It is unnecessary to dwell on the colossal stupidity
of fighting Englishmen by murdering their women
and children.   It may well have lost Germany the
war; for until the passion of hatred was aroused, we
had no bitter feelings against our enemies.   The
state of cold fury in which the nation remained from
that time till the armistice, and unfortunately still
longer, was good for the Allies, but not favorable to
religion.   The clergy themselves were swept away by
it; and the few who ventured to protest could not get
a hearing.   It was indeed necessary for the government to stimulate every force which could increase
the energy and endurance of the nation; and passion-
ate indignation against the enemy was one of the
forces on which they relied.   War mentality is a
strange fever of the spirit; the passions of which at
other times we are ashamed are artificially excited
and turned into one channel; for the time being, the
minds of all are partially unhinged and incapable of
seeing any other colour except red.

Meanwhile, a widespread feeling found frequent

utterance, that the war had proclaimed the final
bankruptcy of the Christian religion. The same
type of persons who asked why God allowed the
sinking of the *Titanic* now asked more persistently
why God did not stop the war. Those who were
better educated acknowledged a bitter disillusion,
not so much because war had broken out—for they
knew that this was possible—but at the extreme
barbarity with which it was conducted. It had been
almost a commonplace that the progress of the race
was shown especially in the increasing humanity of
man to man. A long peace had made our countrymen in particular unfamiliar with the horrors of war,
so that even legitimate operations were a shock to
them; much more were they horrified at the excesses
of the Germans, which, in the well-considered opinion of Lord Bryce, had had no parallel in Western
Europe since the wars of religion three hundred
years ago. Belief in progress, which had been an
article of faith with the majority, was rudely
assailed. It was a further shock to read the utterances of the German clergy, who not only championed
a cause which to us seemed indefensible, but outdid
the politicians in venomous ebullitions of race hatred.
And so the cry was raised, and echoed naturally by
the numerous enemies of organised Christianity, that
the churches had been found out, and that the

impotence of Christian ideas to purify the characters or to moderate the passions of men had now been demonstrated.

This feeling of bitter disappointment was, I think, quite justified. There had been nothing in modern history to prepare our minds for the appalling ferocity of this conflict. All through the eighteenth century we find men noting with complacency the growing humanity with which warfare was conducted. In the Napoleonic war, it is true, we denounced the cruelties of the French in Switzerland; but manifestations of chivalry and mutual respect between the combatants were the rule. About the middle of the long war the French government offered a medal for electrical research, and awarded it to an Englishman, Sir Humphry Davy, who went to Paris to receive it. In 1813 he and Faraday actually lectured in Paris. How inconceivable such an incident would have been in 1916! There is something which has not yet been explained in the outbreak of savagery which accompanied the outbreak of the late war, and which found its first victims in the helpless Belgians, who had certainly given the Germans no cause for violent hatred. Cruelty was by no means confined to one side; but it is surely significant that our soldiers, as I can testify from personal conversations, spoke of the Turks almost with affection as "clean fighters," compared with the enemies whom they encountered on the Western front. The conduct of the war was in truth a reproach to Christendom.

And yet a student of history should know better than to lay these explosions of fanatical nationalism at the door of our religion. In the middle ages the idea of a comity of nations under the Holy Catholic Church and the Holy Roman Empire produced a customary international law which often mitigated both the ambitions of princes and the barbarism of their followers. It was the breakdown of this system which led to modern nationalism; and we can date the beginning of the pernicious doctrine of the God-State by the appearance of Machiavelli's *Prince*. It was Machiavelli who first enunciated the doctrine which Bernhardi developed for the German militarists: "Where the safety of the country is at stake, no consideration of justice or injustice, of mercy or cruelty, of honour and dishonour can find a place. Every scruple must be set aside, and that plan followed which saves the country's life and preserves its liberty."

Machiavelli was a pioneer. Our Francis Bacon professes the same creed: his international ethics differ in no way from the principles expounded before and during the war by German professors. Hobbes, too, says quite plainly that the state can do no wrong. Fichte, in his famous lectures at Berlin after Jena, proclaims the unlimited right and duty of every nation to destroy its neighbours: "No state strives to preserve the balance of power except as a *pis aller*, and because it cannot compass its own aggrandisement or carry out its implicit plan for an universal monarchy. Every state defends the balance of power when it is attacked by another, and prepares in secret the means by which it may in its own time become itself a disturber of the peace. The well-known advice, threaten war that you may have peace, is equally valid in the converse, promise peace in order that you may begin war with an advantage in your favour. Always without exception the most civilised state is the most aggressive."

So, according to the modern theory, history is to remain for all time a dismal conjugation of the verb to eat, in the active and passive. *Civitas civitati lupus*. Fichte's more influential follower, Hegel, calls the state "this actual God," and says that "the state is the divine will as the present Spirit unfolding itself into the actual shape and organisation of the world." Here then is the philosophy, the religion, which has borne this poisonous fruit. Here is the devil's doctrine which has plunged the world in mourning. It is the doctrine which deifies the state, and declares with Hobbes that "there is no power on earth which can be compared with it." The war, with all its horrors and barbarities, is the *reductio ad absurdum* of a false and immoral political theory which took its rise at the time of the Italian Renaissance, and gradually spread over Europe. Will anyone argue that this theory of the state has any connection with Christianity, a religion for which there is neither Greek, nor Jew, "barbarian, Scythian, bond nor free"?

But the vast majority of my countrymen were not thinking or talking but acting. In the midst of our distress at the serious symptoms of social disease at the present time, we must not forget the splendid record of the nation while it was fighting for its existence. We must not forget the heroism of the army and navy in the face of horrors unknown before, the general willingness to serve, the stubborn determination to see the business through, the noble response of the women to the new calls upon them, the readiness of the rich to surrender their comforts and lend their houses to the nation, the patient endurance of anxiety and the gallant courage under bereavement. We have no wish to boast of "England's effort"; it is better to leave our actions to the impartial verdict of history. That verdict will, I believe, be that no more extraordinary exhibition of energy and resolution has ever been recorded than that by which an unmilitary nation, quite unprepared for war, mobilised over nine millions of men, financed its allies, supplied them with munitions, and policed the high seas. A French admiral once said to Napoleon: "Sire, you are better off than I am. You can make a soldier in six months, but it takes six years to make a sailor." "Taisez vous," replied the Emperor angrily, "that is the way empires are lost. It takes six years to make a soldier." An Anglican bishop, calling at the War Office at Berlin for leave to visit English prisoners, told me that the high official who signed the passport said to him: "You know we are amazed at what you English have done in raising your army. We thought it impossible." The fact that the Americans performed the same miracle does not impair the force of the point which I am now urging—that the effort made during the war was so prodigious that a severe reaction was to be expected.

Year after year the war dragged on. The two sides were so evenly matched that no one could be sure that a decision was in sight. In the interests of civilisation during the next fifty years this prolonged death-grapple was perhaps more disastrous than a victory for the aggressors would have been.

Neither side dared to give in; both felt, "It is either our life or theirs." The anxiety was intense and sustained. No one knew whether London might not be reduced to ashes by incendiary bombs; whether Paris might not fall, and the French be driven to capitulate; whether Germany had not some diabolical weapon of wholesale destruction still in reserve; whether some misadventure might not deprive us of the command of the sea and of the means of feeding our population. The frequent air raids on London, of which we tried to make light, were the most nerve-shattering experiences that can be conceived. I soon found that I could not stand it for my family, and sent my young children away into the country. But how many there were who could not do this, and who, after a hard day's work in a munition factory, went home to a broken night's rest, with the possibility that their families and homes might be wiped out in a moment!

The hope deferred that maketh the heart sick was ours again and again. We were hopeful till the time when Russia deserted us, Russia the "steam-roller," whose power we, like the Germans themselves, had so greatly over-estimated. That great empire fell quickly into a state of septic dissolution and utter savagery; only a corner of the curtain has yet been lifted which veils the most hideous tragedy in modern

history.   Then at last America made up her mind to
save Europe from suicide; and from that time the
issue, though long deferred, could hardly be doubtful.
Yet there were few in England who realized in
July, 1918, that the terrible strength of the German
military machine was at last broken.   We thought
that the pendulum had swung again, and that the
winter might find the armies still near the lines of
1915.   By degrees it became apparent that the
struggle was over; that the endurance of the Central
Powers had been stretched to the breaking-point.
The defection of Bulgaria revealed the truth even to
our pessimists, and in a few days more the end came.

The combatants laid down their arms.   There was
a brief expression of devout religious thankfulness for
our deliverance, and millions of parents and wives
drew a deep breath of relief after an almost intolerable strain of anxiety.   Then came the humiliating
spectacle of the Paris negotiations.   In moments of
desperation, the Allies had made promises to certain
nations, in order to bring them into the war, promises
which ought never to have been made, and which, if
they were carried out, could only be the seed of
future wars.   The people of this country did not
show the magnanimity which after our other wars
has stood us in good stead politically as well as
morally.   At the general election of 1919 the party

managers of the coalition thought it good policy to placard the streets with "Hang the Kaiser," and "Make Germany pay." It is an episode which Englishmen will be glad to forget. It was a great misfortune that at this time we had no high-minded statesman to lead the nation. Either Gladstone or Salisbury would have saved us from some disastrous blunders, and would have prevented the sordidness of the peace from staining the memory of a glorious war. The moral temperature of the nation fell rapidly during last year, and the shifts of a tricky and opportunist government were largely responsible for the fall. Little could be expected from a Parliament elected in a paroxysm of greed and vindictiveness. A former Prime Minister told me that the present House of Commons [in 1921] is on a lower level, intellectually and morally, than any other within his experience.

The economic sequelæ of the war have perplexed and astonished our financiers. Anyone visiting this country would suppose that we had come into a vast fortune instead of having lost one. There is every appearance of abundant and widely diffused prosperity. The ruined classes have retired out of sight; they have no friends and no hope; the new rich are flaunting their gains, and the workingman, who was meditating revolutionary schemes when the war broke out, finds himself in a position to hold a pistol at the head of society, and to make constantly increasing demands which the government, destitute of all moral authority and in terror of revolution, concedes as soon as they are made. Democracy is at an end in England; we are at the mercy of predatory gangs who dictate their terms to the government and then tear them up, sending in fresh requisitions. In a country like England, which depends for its existence on foreign trade, there can be only one end to this state of things. We have ruined our best customers, and we apparently wish to keep them ruined. The savings of the half-century before 1914 have already mostly disappeared. The vast sums invested in railways have been partially confiscated by the employees of the lines; the enormous investments in foreign government bonds are now worth very little. We are at present in the position of a young spendthrift made happy by the Jews; we shall soon be in a position to digest George Meredith's poem *The Empty Purse*. A long and bitter period of acute distress, beginning with a great outbreak of unemployment, lies before us. The orgy of lavish spending will probably come to an end in a few months, and the government will be unable to meet the liabilities which it has recklessly assumed.

What will be the results of adversity upon the character of the nation? It is very difficult to prophesy. Hitherto, the Englishman has shrunk from violent revolution. He is a kindly, good-natured fellow at bottom, with a tendency to conservatism and a distrust of heroic remedies. There is in the nation a fund of political common sense and a comparatively high standard of political education. Labour movements are notoriously most aggressive when wages and prices are rising; it is much easier to strike for an increase than to arrest a fall. On the other hand, the country is over-populated; the urban population, which is far more than half the nation, is rigorously dependent upon our ability to exchange our manufactures for imported food. If we lose our foreign trade—and we must lose it, if the workingman goes on behaving as he is doing now—we shall be faced with starvation, and *nescit plebes ieiuna timere*. It is impossible to tell whether we shall go to pieces in futile civil strife, or whether we shall brace ourselves to the arduous and thankless task of recuperation and reconstruction. It is, of course, possible that we shall not be left to work out our own salvation or perdition without interference. The Germans are good haters, and Russia is ready for a Napoleon.

I have little doubt that the lean years will produce

a genuine religious revival.   The bankruptcy with
which we are threatened is moral and social as well as
economic.   We have been nursed on a false theory
of progress, a theory which is false in two ways.   We
have supposed it to be automatic, a kind of law of
nature; and nature has no such law.   We have also
measured it by quantitative standards.   We have
gloated over tables of statistics; we have rejoiced to
hear that our population and our trade and the area
of our empire are growing.   We have even assumed
that this expansion is a proof of the favor of heaven,
and have contrasted our fortunes with those of other
nations—"lesser breeds without the law."   However, it would be very unjust if Americans were to
suppose that great arrogance is characteristic of the
Englishman to-day; it reached its zenith in the days
of Lord Palmerston and Macaulay's History.   We
are not now, I think, an arrogant nation.   But
the vulgar quantitative estimate of good and evil
still remains to warp our judgments, and infects with
materialism our standards of living.

If, as I think probable, we are about to enter on
the path of decline in material wealth, we shall begin
to revise our standards.   We shall realise that we
have been following the wrong road; that our concentration on the good things of this world has not
only failed to bring us happiness, but has led to the

loss of those good things themselves. It seems to be a historical law that no nation remains very rich for a long period. The love of pleasure becomes too strong for the love of accumulation; the tendency to indolence which is innate in human character is no longer checked by want; the different classes in the community begin to fight each other for their share of the spoils; and the expense of protecting the national wealth against acquisitive neighbors becomes a burden too great for the state to bear. Such has been the fate of other wealthy communities; and we are hardly likely to escape it. If we do not escape it, there will be an apparent change in our national character. I say apparent, because it may be doubted whether nature intended the Englishman to be a money-making animal. Behind the practical activities and strength of will which have impressed foreigners as our national characteristics, there is a strong vein of idealism, which has found expression in a very noble poetry, and in the genuine piety of the most typical Englishmen.

It may well be that now that our mission as a world power is nearly accomplished—for we may hope that the young Englands beyond the seas will soon be strong enough to protect themselves—we may realise another and not less worthy ambition, that of being the spiritual home and ancestral hearth

of a number of vigorous nations, speaking our language and moulded on our traditions. Whether this
will be so will depend on the temper in which we
meet the trials of the next fifty years. Are we
ready to welcome a new outpouring of the spirit, if
such should be granted us? An Englishman who
loves his country will hope, but not without many
misgivings. We are being rocked on a turbid stream,
and it is not easy to feel sure whether the current
is bearing us to weal or woe. Just now the populace
is seen at its worst; it is waxing fat and kicking;
but adversity may bring out a better side, as we
found when our prospects in the war looked black.
I am no optimist; but I cling to the faith of Wordsworth's sonnet, composed when we were at death-
grips with Bonaparte:

> It is not to be thought of that the Flood
> Of British freedom, which, to the open sea
> Of the world's praise, from dark antiquity
> Hath flowed, "with pomp of waters, unwithstood,"
> Roused though it be full often to a mood
> Which spurns the check of salutary bands,
> That this most famous Stream in bogs and sands
> Should perish, and to evil and to good
> Be lost for ever.

1921.

V

PSYCHOLOGY AND THE MYSTICS

(I)

THE centre of gravity in religion has shifted from authority and tradition to experience. The evidences of religion are no longer external and miraculous; they are those which faith itself supplies. For example, the apologists of the past invited us to believe that Christ is risen, which is what we want to know, by marshalling the evidence that He rose. The believer to-day, whether he knows it or not, infers that Christ rose, because he feels and knows that He is risen. In his humble measure he can say with St. Paul, "It pleased God to reveal His Son in me."

This change in the centre of gravity in religion has led to a revived interest in what is called mysticism. This unhappy word is encrusted with alien associations, among which, it can hardly be doubted, is a subconscious and absurd association with the idea of London fogs. Mysticism, in philosophy, means the claim that the human spirit can enter into immediate communion with superhuman spirit, not necessarily the Christian God, or the Spirit of Christ, but some living spiritual power above itself. As Christians, our interest is naturally directed to the Christian mystics; but there has been much mysticism of a semi-pantheistic kind among the poets, and there is a great school of philosophy which culminates in mysticism, though its lower stages are rationalistic. There is an extraordinary similarity in the writings of all mystics, even when they belong to different ages, countries, and religions.

Until twenty-five or thirty years ago it was customary to speak of the mystics with amusement, pity, or contempt, an attitude which appears even in the half sympathetic study of the subject by R. A. Vaughan. It is now much more widely recognised that prayer is the mystical act *par excellence*, and that to disparage mysticism is to disparage the devotional life.

But the revival of the study of mysticism is mainly due to the new science of psychology. The phenomenon of mysticism is a challenge to the principles on which this science is based. It calls for an explanation on psychological lines. And since most of the literature upon mysticism is written by psychologists, it is important to understand what the presuppositions of this science are.

But first I will point out that the psychological study of religion came after a naturalistic and purely evolutionary method, which has still many able exponents. Under the influence of Darwin's discoveries it was believed that the way to explain anything was to trace its pedigree back as far as possible. The old heralds gave Adam a coat of arms; modern genealogists give him a coat of fur, and possibly a tail. The tree was to be known by its roots, not by its fruits; the "nature" of anything was not, as Aristotle thought, to be sought for in its complete development, but in the condition out of which its development began. So the "nature" of religion was investigated in the manners and customs of savages, of whom earlier travellers had been content to report, "Manners they have none, and as for their customs, they are beastly." We were taught that religion is essentially a matter of magic, spells, and incantations, and that what we call the higher religions are refined, rationalised, and disguised developments of these primitive superstitions. By the same arguments it might be proved that science grew out of much the same roots, and art out of mere sensation of pleasure and displeasure.

The real lesson of anthropology is that religion, science, ethics, and æsthetics have all become differentiated out of the confused muddle in which they exist together in the mind of the savage. Each branch of human activity has drawn apart and formulated its own laws, without which process it could not understand itself. The next problem is to understand the relations of these subjects to each other, for their separation, though necessary, is, after all, artificial. The study of primitive man has been very valuable, but a bad philosophy has been mixed with it. By their fruits, not by their roots, we shall know what these things are worth.

Psychology owes less to this evolutionary school than to the theories of knowledge which have been agitating the waters of philosophy ever since Kant. Psychology is the study of mental states as such. There are, of course, many thinkers who believe that we can never get beyond mental states as such. They would say that the validity of science and religion consists in their relation to human needs; if it has any relation to absolute truth (assuming "absolute truth" to have any meaning) we cannot know it and need not trouble ourselves about it. This philosophy is popular among psychologists; it exalts their own science by ruling out metaphysics.

But we ought to realise, what they do not always realise themselves, that they are ruling out the foundations or presuppositions of the very convictions which they are investigating when they study religion and mysticism. Psychology cannot do justice to mysticism because the validity of the mystic's faith lies outside its province, and the methods of psychology almost require it to assume that it has no validity, apart from its purely subjective interest to the devotee's own mind. The psychology of the mystical experience may be and is very interesting to the student of mental science. To the mystic himself his experiences are of no interest or value whatever, except as visions of objective reality not created by his own imagination. He may be right or he may be wrong in believing that he has a glimpse of the world beyond the veil; my point is that the psychologist is almost bound to assume that he is wrong. The admission of real inspiration from above would oblige him to admit into his science a whole range of values which he has excluded from consideration; it would destroy his hope of bringing all mental states under a closed system.

Accordingly, since the psychologist has debarred himself from explaining mysticism by philosophy (in the older sense), he is practically obliged to explain it by pathology. Even in William James' famous book, *Varieties of Religious Experience*, there is a tendency to take the abnormal as the typical, and to classify the life of devotion as an unnatural

and unhealthy state of mind. Other writers **have**
gone much further, and I think it should be recognised that this is one of the most insidious **and**
dangerous attacks which religion has now to meet.
It is easy to show that many of the saints have been
neurotic; that they have suffered from the effects
of protracted nervous tension; that extreme concentration on the development of their spiritual
faculties has made them queer and unfit for life
in the world. Many of them have certainly been
subject to hallucinations and fits of misery for which
there was no external cause; the life of the cloister
is not healthy or natural. But this is no excuse for
condemning mysticism as an aberration due to sex-
repression, as some have done. The greatest mystics
—which does not mean those who are visionaries and
nothing else—might have defied even a mad-doctor
to do his worst. Plato, Plotinus, Eckhart, Teresa,
Wordsworth, and Tennyson were all mystics, in
different degrees; and they were all sane and healthy
persons.

Yet we now have psycho-analysts explaining the
consciousness of sin as the result of what they call
the Œdipus complex, and trust in God as a reversion
to the feelings with which an infant regards his
father. The tendency if not the object of these
fanciful and unpleasant explanations is to eliminate

the religious feelings altogether; and they rest on an unjustifiable confusion of normal with abnormal mental states. Religion, so far from being a disease, is essential to mental health, and if we may trust those who in other fields would be called experts in their subject, there is one thing of which they feel increasingly certain, and that is that in prayer and meditation they are actually in contact with a spiritual reality which is not a projection of their own thought and will. It is almost ludicrous that some of the new school try to explain this experience as a variety of auto-erotism or Narcissism, a concentration of sensuous desire upon the self. There is no apparent connection whatever between the two.

Next week I hope to show that recent research has helped to vindicate the mystical experience, which is the core of all personal religion.

VI

PSYCHOLOGY AND THE MYSTICS

(II)

In my article last week I tried to show that the defenders of religion, as the supreme reality in human life, cannot rely entirely on psychology. Psychology is a limited science, dealing with states of mind as such; it cannot, without stepping outside its province, discuss the relation of our mental states to ultimate reality. Questions of mental health and disease do interest psychologists, and they may speak of true beliefs as opposed to false; but by this they can only mean healthy mental conditions as opposed to pathological hallucinations. Intense religious conviction is a masterful mood, which often sweeps away the power of distinguishing between observed fact and imagination. This is notoriously the case in what are called mystical phenomena. The visionary feels as if he were caught up into the air, and sometimes believes that his body has actually been lifted from the ground, which, of course, is a delusion. The psychologist stamps these beliefs as pathological, and the consciousness of union with God which the mystic has actually experienced is tacitly set aside as purely subjective, since the psychologist cannot accept such communion without confessing the inadequacy of his own categories. It comes to this, therefore, that while the naturalists of the last century regarded the material world alone as real, and the spiritual as a dream, psychologists tend to regard science and religion alike as instruments which help us to live. "Whatever helps us is true," as one of them has said; truth, for this school, has no other meaning.

There are, according to the accepted classification, three attitudes, which the mind may take up towards the world. We desire to know our environment and our relation to it; this may be called the cognitive attitude. We desire to enjoy the beauty and harmony and sublimity of the world; this may be called the æsthetic attitude. And we desire to achieve all of moral goodness that we can attain to in our conduct. This may be called the ethical attitude. Theistic philosophers usually say that the objects of these three quests—Truth, Beauty, and Goodness—are the three attributes under which God has revealed His nature and character to man. They are like a triple star in the spiritual firmament, or like the "threefold cord that is not quickly broken"; for, though they cannot be reduced to a single formula, they "never can be sundered without tears," as the poet says.

The question has been endlessly discussed which of these three "faculties" is the organ of religious belief. Is faith a matter of the intellect, or of the æsthetic faculty, or of the will? The schoolmen of the Middle Ages were divided; some championed the intellect, others the will. Modern philosophy is no nearer to an agreement. Besides the rationalists and the voluntarists, there is a third school which regards faith as a product of the æsthetic imagination. Others point out that this "faculty psychology" is out of date; that these different attitudes are not mutually exclusive; and that our convictions, whether scientific, artistic, or ethical, are the result of the reaction of our environment as a whole upon our personality as a whole. The whole man is concerned in his religion, and the intensity and consistency of his belief depends on the degree in which he has succeeded in unifying and disciplining his character.

The only deficiency in this view is that there seems to be something distinctive in the religious attitude, which is neither purely cognitive, æsthetic, nor ethical, nor a blend of these three. We may have known men who display in their characters an admirable combination of scientific interest, artistic taste, and moral earnestness, and who in spite of this are not exactly religious. It is this which has caused the very great attention which has been paid to a recent work by Otto, a German philosopher and theologian, who has also an unusual knowledge of recent natural science. The book is called *Das Heilige*—the conception or idea of the Holy. No book is at present more eagerly discussed in theological circles.

Otto is in partial agreement with Schleiermacher, who found the root of religion in a feeling of absolute dependence, but who did less than justice to the feeling of union with God, which is joined with the feeling of alienation from Him to produce the typical religious attitude. Otto shows that out of the feeling of absolute dependence arise other feelings—a peculiar sentiment of awe, a consciousness that we are in the presence of something at once mysterious, majestic, and fascinating. He sums up these feelings in a word which is not yet intelligible to English readers—a consciousness of the *Numinous* (from the Latin *numen*, divine power). Otto claims that in this attitude we have a definite form of experience, a distinct mode of experiencing reality.

Psychology will, naturally, dissect and analyse this experience, like the others, and will very likely have recourse to the subliminal consciousness, on which much that is wise, and more that is unwise, has been said. To me, the interest of Otto's book is that it raises again the question of a mystical faculty, distinct from the cognitive, æsthetic, and ethical attitudes already mentioned. It is a sound principle not to multiply hypotheses unnecessarily, and though I believe absolutely that the mystical experience is a true, healthy, and normal experience, it seems to me to be closely bound up with the reason, imagination, and moral will. I object particularly to Otto's repeated assertion that faith is essentially "irrational." Even if he does not mean all that the word conveys to English ears, the phrase is unfortunate and misleading. The function of the reason is to co-ordinate the impressions which come to us from various sources; and if reason is excluded from criticising the feelings of awe, majesty, mystery, and fascination which the contemplation of the idea of God arouses, there is no check upon what the Germans call *Schwärmerei*. What I think Otto means to emphasise is that the sense of the Numinous, as he calls it, is something direct and immediate, an experience and not an inference; and this is the postulate of mysticism.

The mystic always finds it difficult, if not impossible, to describe what he has seen and felt. An experience recollected is not the same as an experience felt. It came to him without words and images, more impalpable than the impression of a sunset. If he wishes to make it available for other people, he must reconstruct and interpret and translate, as it were, into another language. It by no means follows that what he has felt has no evidential value except to himself. In fact, the evidence, though halting and sometimes turbid, is extraordinarily unanimous and impressive.

The mystical experience seems to those who have it to transport them out of time and place and separate individuality. This, of course, brings us at once among the most formidable philosophical problems. Those mystics who are also philosophers generally hold that neither space nor time is ultimately real. They may look with favour on Professor Alexander's theory that time is a fourth dimension; they are less likely to agree with Bergson, who gives a supreme metaphysical value to *la durée*. They are also, as a rule, opposed to very rigid doctrines of personality. Personality to them is a fluid concept. They accept St. Paul's tripartite psychology of body, soul, and spirit, and they think of salvation as an elevation of soul into the realm of spirit, where individuality, as we know it, is transcended. Something of this kind they seem themselves to have experienced in their moments of vision.

I have not written with any intention of disparaging the researches into mysticism of men like Starbuck and William James, nor even of writers, like Murisier, who treat mysticism as pathological. The subject has never been investigated so thoroughly before, and none would deny that the pathological element is painfully apparent in many of the mystics.   But the favourite American method of the *questionnaire* seems to me of doubtful value. Many people will not answer such questions; many others are incapable of answering them truly; there are some who enjoy answering them, and they are not those whose experiences are the most valuable. But the psychologists have done much by treating mysticism scientifically.   It is only necessary to remember that religion claims to bring us into contact with an absolutely real Being, infinitely above ourselves.   If there is no such Being, or if He is entirely beyond our knowledge, religion is a delusion, and psychology cannot prove it to be more than a useful or comfortable delusion.

1924.

VII

MODERNISM

(I)

CHRISTIANITY, for the historian, is a great river which had its headwaters in Palestine, but received affluents from all sides. Its Founder appeared to His contemporaries as "the Prophet of Nazareth in Galilee." He followed and far surpassed John the Baptist, who revived the old prophetic tradition after a long interval. The function of the prophets had been to preach moral, including social, reform, to denounce idolatry and oppression, to warn their countrymen that national vices must lead to national disasters, and to spiritualise and moralise religion, which was always in danger of becoming external and formal under the domination of the priests and legalists.

These were the main topics of John the Baptist's preaching, and Christ took up his message where he left it. There is no evidence that Christ, during His ministry on earth, attempted to found a new institutional religion. His disciples in Palestine were content to remain orthodox Jews, who obeyed the Law, and, like many other Jews, expected the coming of the Messiah who was to deliver their country. They were distinguished from other Jews by knowing who the Messiah was to be—their crucified Master, who was soon to return to earth in triumph. But this was only the husk, not the kernel of their faith. For the teaching of Christ, as they remembered it, was far more than a patriotic vision. It was a revelation of the most fundamental and universal laws of life.

His teaching gave an entirely new importance in the moral life to love or sympathy, to joy, and to humility. It laid bare for the first time the open secret of the universe: that gain comes from pain, victory from defeat, and the conquest of evil from self-sacrifice. These ideas are indestructible, because they are true; as soon as they are accepted, if they ever are, our various social disorders and troubles will be virtually at an end.

This revelation is the permanent possession of the human race; it only remains to make it effective. But Palestinian Christianity had a short and obscure existence. The Church that converted the Roman Empire was an European, not an Asiatic, religion. Its organisation was Roman, its theology and philosophy were Greek. The Jewish element in

Christianity was only strong enough to impose, after a sharp struggle, the patriotic literature of the Hebrews as part of the authoritative title deeds of the Church.

The greatest of all the crises through which Christianity has passed was its transplantation into the soil of European culture, which was the work of St. Paul's life. The Church then made its choice; it gained Europe and lost Asia. Compared with this momentous development even the Reformation was of secondary importance.

The Reformers believed that they were clearing away a mass of Pagan accretions from Christianity, and that they were returning to the original Gospel. They were really doing the first, but not the second. Latin Christianity was and is a Mediterranean religion. It is the form which Christianity had to take among the subjects of the Roman Empire. When that Empire collapsed, the barbarians collected such civilisation as they were able to assimilate from the wreck of the ancient culture which they had destroyed; and when, about the twelfth century, they began to have a civilisation of their own, they were still under the tutelage of the Catholic Church, which, it is important to remember, represented, however imperfectly, the principle of continuity with a far more civilised past. Medieval and modern Catholicism remained distinctively Latin in type.

But Northern Europe had never been Romanised; and when the northern nations awoke to national and racial self-consciousness, they realised that Mediterranean Christianity did not suit them. They did not wish to be the spiritual subjects of the Bishop of Rome, any more than they wished to be the temporal subjects of an Emperor of Rome. The Reformation was the beginning of the rise of Northern Europe; it marked the end of the supremacy of the Mediterranean peoples. From this uprising came the British Empire, the American Republic, and the colossal duel for world-supremacy between the two greatest of the northern nations.

The North, then, determined to emancipate itself from the Paganised Christianity of the Mediterranean peoples. But the residuum left after the clearance was not, as the Reformers supposed, the original Jewish Christianity. The Gospel was better understood, certainly, when it was stripped of the vestiges of the old religions, which had distorted it almost beyond recognition. But Protestantism is at least as European as Catholicism; it has never had any attractions for Asiatics. The Reformers appealed to the Bible, including the Old Testament, because they needed a make-weight against the infallible

Church to which their opponents appealed, and found it in the infallible Book.

Perhaps they could not have held their own without an absolute authority to appeal to; but it was a great misfortune, as we are now beginning to discover. The Protestant theory of inspiration is quite untenable, and it is doing great harm to the cause of religion. Generations of English people have been made to believe that their hopes in Christ stand or fall with the historical accuracy of the patriotic legends of a tribe of Bedouins. And we cannot any longer believe that these patriotic legends are all historical.

And yet we are very timid and afraid of throwing away the child with the bath-water, as the Germans say. The truth is that the nations of Northern Europe and their offshoots have not yet found the type of Christianity which suits their racial idiosyncrasies. We have been floundering in religion ever since the Reformation, not losing our hold of essentials, but uncertain what kind of superstructure we ought to build upon the foundation.

We are, then, faced with the gigantic task of reconstructing, or, rather, of constructing for the first time, a type of Christianity which is in conformity with the genius of our nation. I repeat that it is not a question of building on a new foundation—

"other foundation can no man lay but that which is laid, even Christ." But the superstructure is no longer watertight; and it needs much more than patchwork repairs.

When we consider the revolution in many departments of knowledge which has taken place in the last two or three generations, we cannot suppose that we shall solve our difficulties by merely going back to the past. Revivals are shallow things. We must frankly admit that a new revelation has been made to our contemporaries through natural science and modern scholarship; and that any scheme of reconstruction which is to have a chance of standing firm must embody the assured results of secular as well as of theological knowledge. The conflict between science and faith, which racked the minds of the nineteenth century, is not a necessary or a permanent condition. It is a transitional phase, a disturbance of equilibrium, due to the rapid and one-sided progress of knowledge in certain directions.

Traditional theology represents not only the religion of the periods when it took the forms in which it afterwards crystallised, but also the science of those periods; and, unluckily, science in those periods was in a very crude and barbarous condition. We have moved a long way from the scientific beliefs of those times, but we are reluctant to cut out the bits of obsolete science which have become encysted in our religion, like a fly in amber.

Nobody now believes that the universe is a three-storeyed building, with the earth in the centre, heaven above, and hell underneath. Medieval theologians seriously suggested that volcanic eruptions were caused by overcrowding in the infernal regions, and that the world would last just long enough to fill with beatified spirits the vacant space in heaven left by the expulsion of the rebellious angels.

Such fancies seemed plausible before Galileo. We have rejected them, but without quite abandoning the notion that heaven and hell are geographical expressions. Popular religion contains much of this exploded science. It troubles the minds of thousands, and alienates thousands more from the religion of Christ, which was assuredly meant to enlist the co-operation of all men of good will.

The name "Modernism" was given by the late Pope to the Liberal Party in his own Church; it seems likely to be applied to Liberal theologians generally. I have not much sympathy with the Catholic Modernists, for reasons which I hope to state next week; and I am not concerned to defend the theories of any particular branch of modernisers. But I am strongly convinced that the cause of religion has little to fear and much to hope from a thoroughly courageous treatment of these questions. The present state of affairs is intolerable. A clergyman is expected to believe, or at least to profess, a variety of opinions, relating to strictly scientific facts, which all educated men know to be absurd, and it is supposed by many that we cannot be Christians unless we believe them. This is to put a stumbling block in the way of faith.

Faith is not, as a schoolboy is reported to have said, "believing what you know to be untrue." It is rather the resolution to stand or fall by the noblest hypothesis. It is an experiment which ends as an experience, a dedication of the intellect as well as the will to the pursuit of all that is true and good.

Personally I am not at all afraid that honest thinking will ever lead us away from Christianity; but some traditional beliefs will have to go. Tertullian, as long ago as A.D. 200, said: "Our Lord called himself the Truth; He never called Himself Tradition." There is no greater disloyalty to the great pioneers of human progress than to refuse to budge an inch from where they stood.

VIII

MODERNISM

(II)

THERE are two classes of persons who criticise theological Liberals with great asperity—those who think that the progress of knowledge has made no difference to the beliefs which it is possible for a Christian to hold, and those who think it useless to buttress up such a rotten structure as the Christian Church.

The former class really plays into the hands of the latter. But the Modernists themselves are sharply divided. The Liberal Protestant and the Liberal Catholic hold very different views on the most important of all questions, the Person of Christ.

There are no doubt some points on which they think alike. They do not wish to build anything on the literal truth of miracles. It has been said by a German thinker that "miracle is faith's dearest child"; and there is no doubt that many people find comfort in the belief that the laws of nature are sometimes "suspended" by supernatural intervention. Roman Catholics believe that miracles are still of frequent occurrence; they are taught that there are two "orders," the natural and the supernatural, and that these are dovetailed into each other by these wonderful events, which are not so much breaches of law as manifestations of a higher law.

Protestants, who believe that the natural order is now unbroken, still for the most part believe that supernatural portents took place at least once, when the Christian revelation was given. The difficulty which Liberals feel is that since this occasion was admittedly unique, we cannot tell what circumstances were to be expected to attend it. In other words, we cannot tell what amount of evidence is sufficient to establish marvels which, if they were not connected with a Divine revelation, would be rejected without hesitation as unhistorical. It used to be argued that the revelation rested on the miracles; for us it is clear that the miracles rest on the revelation. And we are not prepared to say that the revelation must necessarily have been accompanied by miracles; that would be a generalisation for which we have no data. Arguments from the miracles to the revelation seem to most Liberals to have no cogency.

A very little thought will convince us that miracles,

however well they may be supported, cannot bear the superstructure which has been made to rest upon them. We cannot refute irreligious materialism without disturbing religious materialism at the same time.

Those who wish to understand the profound differences between Protestant Liberalism and Catholic Modernism should read Harnack's *What is Christianity?* and the works of the late Father Tyrrell. Both writers, it is needless to say, are earnest Christians. Harnack lays stress on the teaching of Christ, and on His character. In these he finds a complete and final revelation of the nature and character of God, and of the whole duty of man. This revelation can be studied best in the New Testament itself; for Christianity was afterwards corrupted and mixed up with elements which have nothing to do with the original Gospel. The original gospel is independent of Greek philosophy; but the theology of the Church is built upon the speculations of the later Platonists, and on what the medieval schoolmen believed to be the doctrines of Aristotle.

The Roman Church is, as Hobbes said, the ghost of the Roman Empire; it is a great political institution, utterly unlike the "little flock" which Christ gathered round Him. Our duty, therefore, is to study the character and teaching of Christ, and to apply them to our modern problems, for which they will be found to provide a complete solution.

This has been called "reduced Christianity," and I am far from thinking it sufficient. We cannot do without a philosophy of religion, for philosophy only means thinking things out; and I find the Catholic philosophy, based on the deepest Greek thought, satisfying. Moreover, Harnack does not emphasise the mystical communion with the living Christ, which was the centre of St. Paul's faith; nor does he encourage the inspiring idea of a progressive revelation. But, in spite of these limitations, no one can read *What is Christianity?* without gaining increased insight into the essential message of the New Testament to modern men and women.

Catholic Modernism follows very different lines. Its protagonist, the Frenchman Alfred Loisy, attacked the German Harnack with a vigour begotten of patriotic ardour as well as intellectual conviction. The Liberal Protestant Christ, he declares, never existed. The historical Jesus is a character who refuses to be modernised. He was an enthusiast, a kind of Mahdi, who had nothing new to teach his contemporaries except that "the Kingdom of Heaven," which meant a supernatural destruction of the existing world-order, was at hand.

He went to Jerusalem, not to die, but because

he thought that his Messianic kingdom was about to begin. From this strange episode, according to Loisy, began the great Christian Church, which took Christ as its Saviour-God, much as the rival cults of the Roman Empire worshipped Serapis or Mithra. The growth of the Church was determined by its environment; it had to take various successive shapes in order to survive.

The Catholic Church is very unlike the original Gospel. But what of that? "If you want to prove the identity of a grown man, you do not try to squeeze him into his cradle." We may assume that the Church is what God meant it to be, since we cannot suppose that He meant it to die out, and it would have died out if it had not developed in this way. All the accretions which Harnack wishes to get rid of are adaptations to human needs, and this is their adequate justification. The Catholic Church is a great and successful institution; the religion of Protestant philosophers suits nobody except themselves.

Loisy seems to have thought for a time that he was a defender of French Catholicism against the Boches. But his Church would have none of his apologetic, and roundly denounced it as "a compendium of all heresies." It would have been strange if they had taken any other view, and Loisy is probably much happier as a lay professor. Father Tyrrell presents us with the same philosophy of history, very much watered down; but the Roman Church could not tolerate even Loisy and water.

There are a few able representatives of this school in the Anglican Church; I should be sorry to see their number increase.

Speaking for myself—and a Liberal theologian must speak for himself, since we are not a party—I could not call myself a Christian if I thought that Christ was the deluded prophet of Loisy's commentaries, or that the moral teaching of the Gospels contains nothing new or nothing of unique value.

Some years ago I had the curious experience of being consulted by a Bishop about one of his clergy who had been reported to him for heresy, and in the same week by a Society which wished to know whether, in my opinion, they ought to defend this same clergyman against his Bishop. Both sent me copies of several sermons on which the charge of heresy was based. After reading the sermons, I had no hesitation in advising the society not to take up the case, and the Bishop to get the man out of his living, if possible. Christianity means belief in the historical Christ, and the unlucky man whose attempts to preach an Easter course were sent to me was trying to make bricks without straw, or rather out of straw and nothing else.

I fully admit that in the last century the figure of Christ was too often draped in modern clothes. I am well aware that the Church has incorporated Greek philosophy, much of the old mystery religions, and other elements for which there is no warrant in the Synoptic Gospels. So far, the Catholic Modernists are right. But I think that their picture of Christ as an apocalyptic dreamer is utterly untrue. Loisy's Christ is a psychological monster. Such a character could not have existed, still less could he have founded a world religion.

An honest and reverent study of the New Testament will, I am convinced, lead us to accept the orthodox view that in Christ "dwelleth all the fullness of the Godhead bodily." For a perfect revelation of the Divine under human conditions must be a revelation of goodness, not of power. This is a principle which perhaps carries us further than most of us have yet realised.

This is not the place for theological discussions. I only wish to plead that Churchmen who think for themselves are not traitors in the camp; that they wish, not to destroy, but to rebuild what needs reconstruction; and that in a healthy religious society it is desirable that every man should be encouraged to profess that part of the truth which he sees most clearly. For in a great Church all types of mind are represented. Some see one side of the truth, some another, and all sides should be freely expressed.

The great debates will go on as long as men's minds are active. Are those alone to be silenced whose life's work is to teach, or can anyone teach who is not himself a learner to the end?

1921.

IX

NATIONALISM AND CHRISTIANITY

PROFESSOR McDOUGALL, the eminent psychologist, who in his last book *Ethics and Some World Problems*, has handled questions of political philosophy in an interesting, if not always convincing manner, finds the main cause of the conflict of ideals within European civilisation in two divergent codes of ethics, which the Western peoples have vainly attempted to combine. Europe has oscillated between the universal ethics taught by Christianity and the nationalist ethics which have survived and flourished in spite of the principles and precepts of our religion. This disharmony of moral practice has given a powerful stimulus to thought and discussion, and has indirectly led to a diffusion of the Western races and their culture, for emigration has often been the result of religious or secular coercion. On the other hand, it has caused constant unrest, and has several times deluged Europe with blood.

The Professor further argues that while the principles of universal ethics have been generally and explicitly accepted, the principles of nationalist ethics have remained unformulated and unacknowledged, so that demands made in the name of the nationalist principle have been shamefaced and apologetic. He thinks that there is a danger lest the universal ethics of Christianity, which in spite of their attractiveness, lead in practice to stagnation and at last to national decay, may prevail over nationalist ethics, which though liable to perversion, as the example of Germany proves, give the only hope of health and progress. He therefore pleads for a sound, vigorous, and scientific nationalism, and exhorts us to dismiss cosmopolitanism, which he rightly distinguishes from internationalism, as a false and mischievous ideal.

He assumes that Christianity is ultra-democratic in the sense of regarding every human being as equal in value, and anti-national in recognising no difference between Jew and Greek, barbarian and Scythian. On Christian principles, he thinks, every nation would be obliged to open its doors to all comers, and by humanitarian legislation to protect its own weaklings against the effects of competition. After a hundred years, while such principles were in operation, we should find all the new countries densely populated with Chinese, Japanese, Indians and negroes, while among the white races dysgenic selection would have played havoc with the moral, intellectual, and physical qualities of the populaton. The application of "universal ethics" will therefore end by destroying modern civilisation, as, in the judgment of our author, it undermined the civilisation of antiquity.

Professor McDougall seems to be influenced by Naumann, a militarist though a Christian, who apparently wishes to recognise the double code, but to apply it to different parts of life. Pure nationalism is to direct public affairs, while Christianity is to be accepted as the law for individual conduct. This is precisely the double morality which led Germany to plunge the world into war. No solution is possible on these lines.

There is, no doubt, some plausibility in this interpretation of Christian ethics. The teaching of the Gospel is individual and universal. All that falls between these two extremes is driven into the background. Social and political distinctions are in principle abolished by being ignored. There is next to nothing in the Gospels about our duties as citizens; art and science are not recognised; even the family is spoken of as an interest which may come between the individual and the divine call. The early Christians were accused of *incivisme*, and owed some of their unpopularity to this charge. Celsus, in his lost attack upon Christianity, seems to have urged them not to forget that the Empire was in danger, and needed their loyalty. Even in the recent Great War many persons refused to fight on the same grounds which kept the early Christians out of the army, and if there had been more of them we should now have German "Field-greys" swaggering in Piccadilly.

Nevertheless, I think the Professor is wrong. The original Gospel contemplated no future for the Church, which was a mere stop-gap till the Kingdom of God should come. But as soon as the new religion passed into Europe, it organised itself with a facility which would have been impossible if it had been intrinsically as politically inert and quietistic as the Buddhism of Burma. The Roman Government persecuted the Church not as a company of world-renouncing ascetics—there were many such "philosophies" in the Empire, which excited no hostility. It attacked the Church as something much more dangerous, a closely-knit and ambitious corporation, which aimed at establishing an *imperium in imperio*, the unpardonable sin under an autocracy. The Church was not anti-national; it fostered a nationalism of its own. More and more as time went on the Kingdom of God became a kingdom in, if not of, this world, and gathered around it all the sentiments and emotions of aggressive patriotism.

At the beginning of the modern period, when the nations of Western Europe became conscious of their organic unity and right to independence, some of them revolted against the centralised theocracy which preserved under a new form the methods and traditions of the fallen Empire. But they revolted, not against cosmopolitanism, but against an alien imperialism. The nature of the resistance offered by the Church showed that the theocratic Cæsar and his prætorians were not reasserting the individualism and universalism of the original Gospel; they were suppressing a political rebellion. The nearest approach to primitive Christianity was not made by the Catholics, nor by the great Protestant Churches. It was left to the step-children of the Reformation, the enthusiastic sectaries.

The rival ideals of which the Professor speaks certainly exist. But they are not the ideal of nationalism and the ideal of Christianity. The anti-national parties—the Kaiser's *Vaterlandslose Leute*—are predominantly anti-Christian, and not merely anti-clerical. Christianity in history has sometimes torn men away from allegiance to the State in the name of another allegiance, equally political. It has never been cosmopolitan or socially disintegrating.

The rival ideals are the individualism run mad, which calls itself Socialism, and the essentially organic theory of society which, as Herbert Spencer saw, is the philosophy of Toryism. Spencer quite erroneously supposed that the social revolution was taking this latter form, which, as a Liberal, he regarded as retrogression. We have, in fact, renounced the political and economic theories which made England the workshop of the world in the last century; but we have renounced them not in favour of a closer and more efficient organisation, but of a reckless squandering of the fruits of industry on "bread and games," without regard to the social value of the recipients. So far as this policy rises above mere election bribery into the region of theory, it is ultra-individualistic. The unit is the individual citizen, who is conceived as sharing an equal claim to material comfort.

From another point of view, the conflict is between the present and the future. The care for the interests of posterity is intelligible only to the educated, and has no place in politics under a democracy. Although the welfare of the people of England a hundred years hence is as important, and as much our concern, as the comfort of our own contemporaries, the practical politician knows that he may safely ignore the rights of those who, being unborn, have no votes.

Christianity is not wholly on either side. It asserts the right of every individual to be treated as a person, who is not to be used up callously in the service of any inhuman machine, military or industrial. But it is not, and never has been, a soft and pleasure-seeking creed. It has borne suffering willingly, and has not been very chary in inflicting it. Its aim is the development of a society composed of perfected men and women, and progress must be intrinsic, not the product of machinery. Rightly understood, it may be a reconciling principle between Socialism and Individualism, ideals which are complementary of each other.

That the nation must be the main object of loyalty I entirely agree. Each nation has its own contribution to make to the commonwealth of humanity, and no other devotion has so great power of calling into activity the best that a man can give. Patriotism needs to be refined and exalted, not to be quenched in deference to some supposed higher cause. There is no limit to the noble aspirations which the words "my country" may evoke.

1924.

X

LIVES OF CHRIST

It remains to be seen whether Papini's *Story of Christ*, recently published in English, will have a sale comparable to the immense popularity of the original work in Italy. Probably it will. Most of the lives of Christ have had a great sale. The public cannot have enough of them.

This is a fact to ponder over. Jesus Christ lived nearly two thousand years ago, in a country which even then was remote from the chief centres of population and culture. The materials for a biography are miserably scanty, and some of these are not scientific history as we understand it. No new documents have come to light, or are ever likely to come to light. The old documents are the most familiar and widely known of all books. Why, then, cannot we be content with the Gospels?

The chief reason is that Christ remains the most supremely interesting figure in all history. Many people have lost faith in the Churches, but only the most violent enemies of society have lost faith in Christ. After 1900 years He still counts for much

more in human life than any other man that has
ever lived. As Robert Browning says:—

That one face, far from vanish, rather grows,
Or decomposes but to recompose,
Become my universe that feels and knows.

It is significant that the great output of Lives
of Christ belongs entirely to the last hundred years.
In spite of the desire of the saints to imitate the
suffering life of the Redeemer, the celestial Christ,
the object of the Church's worship, withdrew attention from the actual human career of Jesus. The
wish to know the facts of that life as they were, to
realise how He lived among the surroundings of an
Eastern land long ago, to picture the climate and
scenery, the manners and customs of Palestine, is a
modern state of mind. The historical sense is, on
the whole, a modern thing. Hence the great popularity of picture-books like Hole's, in which the
scenes were painted on the spot, and of word-paint-
ing like Renan's *Life of Jesus*.

That extraordinary book, the first of its kind in a
Roman Catholic country, where the text of the Gospels is by no means so familiar to the average reader
as in our own land and in Germany, popularised the
critical temper, and created great scandal as well as
immense interest. It is by no means the best of

Renan's works, though the atmosphere of Palestinian life and scenery is most skilfully reproduced.

Renan was deficient in moral seriousness; his portrait of Christ is psychologically impossible, as well as offensive to the believer. He depicts Jesus as "a charming young joiner," who preached a genial message amid idyllic surroundings to admiring women and honest peasants, till He fell under the grim influence of a fanatical prophet, John the Baptist. From that point His character began to deteriorate; He not only became fierce and gloomy, but resorted to deception in pretending to work miracles, notably at the grave of Lazarus. Nevertheless, in the garden of Gethsemane He may still have thought of the girls "who might have consented to love Him"!

The two best comments on this very French romance are that of an educated sceptic who put the book down saying: "*Enfin il était Dieu*," and that of the sentimental young lady who exclaimed, "What a pity it did not end with a marriage!"

Several other books have followed the same lines, without such lapses from good taste. Dr. Edersheim, an Englishman of Jewish descent, was able to illustrate the Gospels from his great store of learning in Jewish customs. Dean Farrar's life won enormous popularity by pleasing but rather sentimental amplifications of the narrative. I remember a schoolboy saying with unconscious irony: "Very little is said about this incident in the Gospels, but a full description may be found in Farrar's *Life of Christ*."

Papini's book belongs to the same class as Farrar's. It is absolutely uncritical; the narratives are taken as they stand in the documents, whether in the Synoptics or in St. John, and amplified with picturesque detail derived either from the writer's imagination or from his first-hand knowledge of the country, which he has studied with the appreciation of a poet and artist. But he is superior to Farrar in his vivid and penetrating interpretation of the character and teaching of the Master, in Whom, after being an agnostic, he has come to believe with all his heart.

Another class of "lives" has come from the critical scholars. Many years of keen analysis have brought to light the different strata in the first three Gospels, and their partial dependence on earlier documents, now lost. After a long controversy, the real character of the Fourth Gospel, as a mystical interpretation of the life of Christ, written for the third generation of Christians, has been placed beyond doubt, though not beyond doubters. This critical labour has led to a further investigation of the position and teaching of Christ in relation to the thought of His time.

A great commotion was made by the theory of Albert Schweitzer, who, in an irritatingly superior tone, declared that all former views of Jesus were erroneous, seeing that He was in reality merely an apocalyptic prophet who went about proclaiming that the world was coming to an end in a few years. Considering that nothing came of this prediction, and that a prophet who stood forward with such a disturbing message might be thought a thoroughly mischievous person, it is strange that Schweitzer himself became a hard-working medical missionary, and that several Christian scholars, including the Roman Catholic Modernists, with whom Pope Pius X. dealt so severely, have persuaded themselves that this theory is not subversive of the Christian faith.   Other critical Lives have been on more conservative lines, omitting the miraculous element, but in other ways conforming to the traditional view of the Galilean ministry.

A third class of Lives is mainly devoted to the moral teaching of Christ, and its meaning for us to-day. These books, which Schweitzer and Loisy despise, are really of great value.   After all, it is this aspect of the narrative which has a living interest for us now. The unavoidable danger is that modern writers tend to modernise Jesus too much, seeking from Him answers to questions which never came within His purview, and trying to enlist His authority on the side of present-day social or even political theories. Christ was certainly not *"le bon sansculotte."* He did not belong to the submerged class, but to a very well-educated, independent, and fairly prosperous class of artisans, farmers, and fishermen. He was not a social revolutionist, hardly even directly a social reformer. The Christian Socialist finds little to appeal to in His teaching; what there is comes almost exclusively from the Gospel of St. Luke. His social message really was, in modern language: "Get your values right, and your institutions will work well enough, or if not they can then be improved without difficulty."

Again, national ideals have somewhat distorted the portraits of Christ. Sir John Seeley's *Ecce Homo*, still a very stimulating book, could hardly have been written except in England. Renan's Jesus is an unmistakable Frenchman. The German Protestant Lives, with their emphasis on the "frank manliness and power" of Christ's character, present us with a half-Teutonised portrait of their hero. But after making deductions for these national prejudices we are left with the impression, after reading these books, that we really know a great deal about Christ. We know Him in the same sort of way in which we know Socrates. There are great gaps in the record: but the salient features in the character and in the teaching are not doubtful. No one need disquiet himself about the extreme sceptical theories of a few scholars, none of them of the first rank, who would have us believe that the historical Christ never existed.

Each generation really adds something to our knowledge of this historical Figure. For, in the words of an early writer, He summed up in Himself all the series of human existence, and this experience deepens with the course of time. A career of universal significance has a special message to each age in turn. We judge it from our own standpoint, and it judges us.

1924.